GLORIFY GOD

———————— ❦ ————————

PORCIA WADE

Contents

INTRODUCTION

"Or do you not know that your body is a temple of the Holy Spirit within you, whom you have from God? You are not your own, for you were bought with a price. So glorify God in your body. " ~ I Corinthians 6:19-20 (ESV)

I am writing this book after years of disobedience. I am writing this book after years of ignoring this very scripture that is the foundation for everything that you will read in this book. If I go back to my early Sunday School years, I remember being taught that I was bought with a price by my Savior, Jesus Christ. No, I was not auctioned off and sold to the highest bidder like my ancestors. My purchase was more extensive and more powerful than that. I was bought by Jesus, a transaction that cost Him His life by the shedding of His blood. I was bought with *His* blood so I could be redeemed and returned to God, my Father, who never wanted me to be lost in the first place. At an early age, I became well acquainted with Calvary's cross and the finished work that was done there.

Shortly after accepting Jesus Christ into my life as a child, I learned that God's Spirit, the Holy Spirit, wants to dwell on the inside of me. With that, I invited the Holy Spirit into my life and asked Him to lead and guide me in my walk with Christ. I would say that overall, my relationship with God has been solid since the days of my youth. I started and led an after-school Bible study club at my high school, I pray and read my word daily, I serve at my church, and I strive to live a life that is pleasing to God.

Still, I found the most significant gap in my relationship with God was the latter part of the above scripture: *"So glorify God in your body."* Like most of you, I read that part and agree with it, but I fail to carry out that stated instruction consistently and thoroughly. And yes, it is an instruction. Glorifying God in our body is not just a good idea or a suggestion; it is a command. Why? The scripture answers that question for us...because we are not our own; we were bought with a price. When someone buys someone or something, the purchaser has authority over what was purchased.

As long as I live in my body on this Earth, my *daily* objective should be to glorify God. Transparently, I lost sight of this daily objective because I have so many other goals and ambitions. I want to be an awesome wife and mom! I want to be everything my husband needs and desires. I want to be reliable and available for my kids. If they are playing in a game, I want to be there. If there is a moment where they fall, I want to pick them up. I always want my kids to know that I love them, I am for them, and I see them. Then there are the personal ambitions I have. I want to experience new opportunities in my career, I always want to learn, I want to vacation, and I want to be healthy and physically fit as I do all of the above.

Transparently, it is hard to be driven in life and deep in God, and maybe that's why we lose focus on what matters most: glorifying God with our bodies every day. Then culture introduces its own set of competing priorities, and we settle for loving God and knowing that He loves us, but we don't glorify God with our bodies. Today, God says, ***I gift you with breath each day, and you must glorify me with your body***. If we are not doing this, we are disobedient, and God's grace for our disobedience is running out. God will not continue to allow us to thrive in our secular lives while His glory suffers. We cannot continue to put off being vessels for Him while we feed our flesh and nourish our narcissism. God needs Christ-followers who will bear the image of Christ and reflect His light in a world that is blinded by darkness.

This book is not a pleasant read; it is a call to action. If you do not want to act, you should not continue to read this book. Every word on every page of this book will call you into accountability and give you instructions on how to be a more promising, potent, and productive believer. If you keep reading this book, you will be compelled to glorify God with every part of your being and experience His glory, presence, and heart in return.

Chapter One

THE PURCHASE

SHOUT OUT TO EVERY Sunday School teacher who taught us this scripture! Many of us learned very early on that our Father in Heaven (God) sent his Son (Jesus) into the world to serve as a sin-sacrifice and Savior for us. However, we need to understand the beginning of mankind and the deadly grip of sin for Jesus' sacrifice to impact and resonate with us genuinely.

Adam was the first human being God created, "The Lord God formed a man from the dust of the ground and breathed into his nostrils the breath of life, and the man became a living being" (Genesis 2:7, KJV). From there, God created Eve, "But for Adam no suitable helper was found. So, the Lord God caused man to fall into a deep sleep; and while he was sleeping, he took one of the man's ribs and then closed up the place with flesh. Then the Lord God made a woman from the rib he had taken out of the man, and he brought her to the man" (Genesis 2:20-21, NIV).

Adam and Eve lived in the Garden of Eden, enjoyed the fruit of the land, and basked in the presence of God until they ate the fruit God forbade them to eat. When they ate the fruit and disobeyed God's instruction, they introduced sin into the beautiful world God created. Once sin was introduced into the world, there was a reproduction of sin with every human that was born after Adam and Eve (Genesis 3). Sin, however, did not stay contained in the narrow lane of disobedience. Adam and Eve's sin gave birth to other sinful desires. Later, their son, Cain, would feel jealousy towards his brother, Abel, and desire to take his life. That desire leads Cain to kill Abel. Cain's act introduced the sin of murder into the world (Genesis 5).

Later on, in Genesis 6, we learn that the sons of God (believed to be fallen angels or demons) had sexual intimacy with the daughters of mankind (the descendants of Adam and Eve), and this sexual intimacy introduced all kinds of sin into the world—sins like perversion, lust, and depravity. Sin overwhelmed the Earth, and it grieved God until He finally said, "My spirit will not remain with mankind forever, because they are corrupt. Their days will be 120 years" (Genesis 6:3, CSB). God decided to reduce the lifespan of His beloved children because of the gestation of sin. God originally intended for men and women to live forever, but He did not want men and women to live in sin forever.

God was devastated because human wickedness was so widespread on the earth and because every inclination of the human mind was nothing but evil at all times. So, God decided to end humanity and start afresh. God chose to begin His new world from the genes of one man He favored, Noah (Genesis 6:5-8). Maybe you know the story of Noah and the Ark; perhaps you do not. In short, Noah heard the Lord tell him to build an ark because rain was coming, and Noah obeyed. God entrusted Noah with His plans to destroy the Earth by flood. The only humans God planned to save were Noah and his family. Noah was also instructed to bring two of every kind of living thing on the ark so they could reproduce their kind in the new world God was going to create.

With that, God destroyed every living creature by way of flood. Water flooded the Earth and consumed all of the Earth's inhabitants except those who were in the ark with Noah. When Noah stepped off the ark and onto the new Earth, he was inclined to plant a vineyard because he was experienced in working the soil. His background was in farming. Noah drank some of the wine from the vineyard he planted, became drunk, and got naked in his tent. Noah's desire to drink the wine of the vineyard (in excess) introduced drunkenness, a form of debauchery, into the new world. Sin was present once again (Genesis 9, KJV).

Why did I spend the last few paragraphs chronicling these Bible characters, the introduction of sin (Adam and Eve), and the reintroduction of sin (Noah)? You must understand why we need Jesus to serve as our Savior and that Jesus is the ultimate sacrifice for our sins. The Bible breaks it down like this, "When tempted, no one should say, 'God is tempting me.' For God cannot be tempted by evil, nor does he tempt anyone; but each person is tempted when they are dragged away by their own evil desire and enticed. Then, after desire has conceived, it gives birth to sin; *and sin, when it is full-grown, gives birth to death* [emphasis added]" (James 1:13-15, NIV).

The end game for sin is death. Yes, a physical death that leads to eternal torment in hell. However, before there is ever a physical death, there is a spiritual death. Adam and Eve were the forerunners and prime examples of what a life with sin looks like. They were expelled from a physical garden, but that expulsion mirrors the separation sin creates between God and His children. To be clear, God did not want distance between Him and His children, but human desires and *decisions* to choose sin fractured the relationship between God and humanity.

Bondage is also included in the spiritual death, 'not-so-prize' package. Earlier, I mentioned the gestation of sin. Gestation, when it comes to a baby, is the process or period between conception and birth when the baby develops inside the womb. Similarly, sin does not stay in seed form; it grows. When it grows, it creates dependencies in various areas of our lives. These dependencies lead to bondage because, before we know it, the "little" sin that we embrace has overwhelmed us, and we begin to pander to it. We work overtime to gratify our sinful desires, we yield to their cravings, and we bow to their demands. That is bondage.

Thank God for Jesus

God sent His son Jesus into the world out of His deep and desperate love for you and me. God was not okay with the fractured relationship between Him and His children. Moreover, He was not content with sin wreaking havoc in the lives of His children or seeing His children experience death because they could not break free from the grip of sin. This is *why* God gave His Son, Jesus. It really is more than a Sunday school lesson. It is more powerful and meaningful than a John 3:16 bumper stick or tattoo. God SO LOVED the world, His creation, His children, the ones that He made in His image, you, and me, and that is why He gave Jesus.

God knew in His infinite wisdom that Jesus was the only suitable sacrifice. I didn't talk to you about the priests of the Bible and how they would go into the Lord's temple to offer burnt sacrifices to God. They did this to atone or make amends for their own sins and the sins of people. They did this to ask for forgiveness (Hebrews 10:11, KJV). The priests' burnt offerings defined a path for forgiveness but did not defeat sin.

Jesus defeated sin! His crucifixion and, more importantly, His resurrection defeated sin! First Corinthians 15: 54-56 (NIV) tells us, "When the perishable has been clothed with the imperishable, and the mortal with immortality, then the saying that is written will come true: 'Death has been swallowed up in victory.' 'Where, O death, is your victory? Where, O death, is your sting? The sting of death is sin, and the power of sin is the law. But thanks be to God! He gives us the victory through our Lord Jesus Christ."

Sin is now impotent, powerless. You might be thinking, *sin has a grip on me, and its grip is firm*! That is a fact. However, the truth is that Jesus defeated sin when He rose from the grave thousands of years ago! He rose with **all** power over sin. That means sin does not have the right or authority to keep you or me in a chokehold because of the finished work of Jesus on the cross. God purchased us on the cross; the price was His Son's blood.

Note that I did not say that we will never sin. We all have sinned and will sin. Romans 3:3 (KJV) tells us, "For all have sinned and fall short of the glory of God." However, there is a difference between committing a sin and being in bondage to sin. When God purchased us, He freed us from the bondage of sin (Romans 6:18).

You may be thinking, *ok, so you are free, I am free, so what?* Great question. We were not freed from sin so we could live our most fabulous, carefree, and God-free lives! No, we were freed from sin's grip and weight to live for God. We were freed to live the set-apart life that God intended for us before He formed us in our mother's womb (Jeremiah 1:5). Freed to walk out the specific steps that God ordered for us (Psalms 37:23). Freed to live the abundant and full life that Jesus promised to us (John 10:10). Freed not just to live, but to be *alive*!

Romans 6:11-14 (NIV) breaks it down like this, "In the same way, count yourselves dead to sin but *alive* to God in Christ Jesus. Therefore, do not let sin reign in your mortal body so that you obey its evil desires. Do not offer any part of yourself to sin as an instrument of wickedness, but rather offer yourselves to God as those who have been brought *from death to life*; and offer every part of yourself to him as an instrument of righteousness. For sin shall no longer be your master, because you are not under the law, but under grace."

Note how Romans 6 tells us that we are dead to sin and *alive* to God in Christ Jesus. It goes on to say to us that we went from death to life. You might be thinking; I have been living my whole life; what *are you talking about?* Truthfully, if you are not *alive* to God in Christ Jesus, you haven't even begun to live yet. Yes, you are breathing. Yes, you are functioning, and perhaps you have even experienced great pleasures in this world; you have had great relationships, achievements, wealth, etc. But when you are *made alive* in Christ, you experience an awakening! Good times outside of Christ are dull because God is light. Life outside of God is laced with this perpetual emptiness; you think "something is missing" or "there has to be more for me" because there is a fulfillment that only comes when you are *alive* in Christ.

You might also be thinking, *why won't God just let me live?* I have also asked this question before. I think we all have. The term "let me live" means leave me be or get off my back. As believers in Jesus Christ, we understand the sacrifice God made for us when He sent His Son to die for our sins. We are even grateful for what Christ did on Calvary's cross and His resurrection from the grave. But still, there is this pervasive thought: *Why is God pressing me? Why can't God accept my gratitude and leave it at that?* We may not verbally say to God, "Why won't you just leave me be or get off my back?" However, whenever we are confronted with the decision to choose God over our desires or hear His call to walk out His plan for our lives boldly, we usually find ourselves frustrated with God. Why? Because we want Him to "let us live," leave us be, and get off our backs, but God will not do that.

God purchased us because He wants us to be alive, and He wants us to live for Him! God is not content with watching His children just live, not after He sacrificed His Son so we can experience relationship with Him and have fruitful lives. Maybe someone told you, or you said to yourself that once you fully submit your life to God; to His will, His purpose, and His plans, God is going to kill your dreams, steal the joy from life, and destroy anything that you have built (career, personal brand, etc.). The truth is that our enemy, the devil, comes to kill, steal, and destroy. Jesus came to give us life in the full (John 10:10). God wants us to dream dreams. He wants us to have joy; as a matter of fact, He fills us with joy (Romans 15:13). God is also the master architect; He builds relationships, careers, and brands way better than you or I could ever build them. Stop believing the lie that living for God means you will miss out on all the good things life has to offer. Scripture tells us that God will not withhold good things from those whose walk is blameless, those who live for Him and are alive in Him (Psalms 84:11).

Not only do we get good things from God, but we also get God. We get to be in a relationship with God [who loves us] and demonstrated that love by paying for us with His Son's blood. We get to talk to and walk with God regularly, who promises to be our peace and covering throughout life. We have 24-hour access to God, who will be our comfort in times of pain, clarity in times of confusion, and our defender in times of adversity. Then, after our earthly journey is over, we will leave this body and be with God for eternity. All of these benefits for the measly asking price that you and I glorify God with our bodies; we acknowledge Him in all our ways and make sure that people know about our great God.

God is simply asking that we go public with the relationship, that we live in such a way that people can see that we are alive in God, and we are not just living like everyday folks who are walking around without God and without hope. Now that we think about it, glorifying God with our bodies is the least we can do.

Yes, when God inserts Himself into your life, and you begin to surrender your will for His will, it will feel very disruptive. God is big, and He wants to take up space in your life. The shift that will happen as you renovate your body (your temple) to make room for Christ may feel chaotic and messy. You will likely see mindsets, behavior patterns, habits, and even some relationships get removed in the demo process. However, God always replaces what He subtracts. And the life God offers you is far greater, more peaceful, and more powerful than life outside Him.

Chapter Two

THE BUILDING

*"For no one can lay a foundation oth-
er than the one that has been laid down.
That foundation is Jesus Christ." ~ I*
Corinthians 3:11 CSB

My HUSBAND AND I started building our first home in August 2020. No, it didn't feel like an ideal time to build a house, given the global pandemic that was underway. We were still shuttering in place, working from home, wearing masks everywhere we went, and attending worship service online, and in the midst of all of the chaos, we started to build our first home. Before I jump into the construction details, I need to walk you back about ten years.

My husband and I got married in May of 2009. The following year (2010), God gave us the desire to own a home. We were renting an apartment at the time, and we were fine with that. We talked about owning a home at some point, likely in the distant future. However, at the present time, we were focused on our new marriage, our growing family, finding jobs that paid well, paying the bills, and carrying out our ministry responsibilities in the church, etc.

But in 2010, God *gave us* the desire to own our own home. We knew it was a God-given desire because it didn't start with us; it wasn't something we were seeking at that moment. Moreover, the desire to own a home wasn't timely or practical. I will spare you all of the financial details, but let's just say our current incomes, growing debt, monthly bills, and daycare fees didn't precisely align with home ownership. Still, God pressed us to shift our minds to home ownership. From there, we started looking at homes in our city and surrounding cities, not just a few homes, like *every* home. We started going to open houses when we saw "For Sale" signs in neighborhoods. We were deeply interested in every new construction community. We would see the developer's tarp around leveled land and begin to inquire about the new homes that were on the way. We would add our names to 'Interested Buyers' lists. We waited patiently for model homes to be built so we could tour the model homes and visit the accompanying sales offices. We became experts in home-buying-speak and learned about down payments, closing costs, interest rates, debt-to-income ratios, and FICO scores.

Between 2010 and 2020, we looked at many (I mean hundreds) of homes on our quest for home ownership. During this time, we applied for home loans and were denied due to our low income and poor credit history. At one point (around 2013), we were approved for a home loan but were approved for a low amount due to our income. They approved us for a home loan, but the loan amount was low, and it wasn't easy to find a suitable home within the price range of our loan approval. A few years later, when our household income increased, we reapplied for home loans, but by then, our FICO scores (credit scores) had taken a hit due to unpaid debts. It was a long and exhausting journey for us to acquire home ownership.

Maybe you are reading this and think *it doesn't take all of that to buy a home; I purchased my house within a matter of six months.* I am glad that was your story, but that was not the story for my family. It was a decade-long pursuit for my family, and God was developing us in the process. He grew us up spiritually and taught us how to trust and depend on Him. He also increased our household income and taught us fiscal responsibility. So, when God directed us to a new construction community in the summer of 2020 and told us we would build our home there, we followed His lead. The timing felt off; a global pandemic ensued, but we trusted God's voice and listened.

We signed the *purchase* order for our new-build home in August 2020. Keep in mind that the last chapter was "The Purchase." When you purchase something, you are declaring ownership. When we signed the purchase order, we declared that a plot of land in Apopka, FL, belonged to the Wade family. The 'Sold' sign went up, and the building permits followed.

Sharp turn, Jesus Christ purchased you, but did the 'Sold' sign ever go up? Have the building permits followed? God did not send His Son to die for you to leave you as a purchased plot of land. What good is dry ground just sitting there packed with potential? God always intended to make His Home in you. The purchase was just the beginning. When you accept the purchase and receive salvation, that is just the beginning. From there, you must declare yourself 'Sold,' off the market, and set apart for God's use. Then the building begins!

My husband and I were so excited when we received the permits from the city of Apopka because that was when the building began on our new home. The very first thing that was laid was the foundation. The foundation was and is the most crucial element of our house. The foundation was an extremely thick cement slab. Foundations have to be firm and strong because they support the entire structure of the home. If you have ever seen home-sites post natural disasters or horrific weather events, the roof, the framing, and the drywall may have been destroyed in the weather incident, but the foundation slab remained.

When God purchased you, He knew that building *you* was His next assignment. He knew that constructing your mind and heart to be like His would be an ongoing project. He understood that His Spirit would need to live inside you, so He would have to make *you* a suitable home. God was not uninformed about the amount of work it would take to make you a temple for Him, a vessel that glorifies Him. But God is *really* confident in the foundation, His Son, Jesus Christ.

The Apostle Paul told us in 1 Corinthians 3:11 (CSB), "For no one can lay any foundation other than what has been laid down. That foundation is Jesus Christ." Paul was speaking to the Corinthian church, which was experiencing division, rejecting God's truth, and becoming increasingly carnal (focused on satisfying their fleshly desires and relying on their human instincts and intelligence instead of God). Paul was calling them to remember their foundation, Jesus Christ.

Our physical home relies on its foundation. Our spiritual home relies on its foundation, which is Jesus Christ. Before you can begin glorifying God in your body, you must ensure you have the proper footing and give God permission to build you up for His purpose and according to His design. I recognize the timing feels off; life is 'lifing', and similar to what my husband and I felt in 2020, the circumstances don't seem right to build. But take God's lead on this one. The timing could not be better; the time is now!

Christ Is Our Firm Foundation

You read the first chapter, "The Purchase," and you know Jesus died for your sins. By now, you understand or are starting to understand, the depths God went through to ensure you could be freed from sin and made alive in Christ. God's desire for a relationship with you is coming into focus, and hopefully, your desire for a relationship with Him is stirring.

However, if you do not *accept* Jesus into your heart, all of this relationship with God and 'glorify God with your body' stuff will be just that, stuff. Jesus went out on a limb(literally) when He gave Himself over to death and was resurrected from the grave. He did all of that as an act of proposal. He gave His life in a gruesome fashion, wrapped Himself in sin, experienced momentary separation from His Father (God), endured the cheers of the enemy, and was resurrected from the grave with the *hope* that you would accept the offer of salvation.

I am always here for a good visual, so visualize this. A man is deeply in love with a woman, and she pays him little to no attention. Still, He caters to this woman; he ensures she has what she needs and her daily provisions are met. He gives her gifts upon gifts, things that he knows she wants and needs. This man is committed to this woman; he is invested in a relationship with her. On the other hand, she is not committed to him; she dates other people. She goes to this man when she needs something but quickly flees to someone or something else once her needs are met. Still, he is so enthralled with this woman that he decides to make it official and marry her. He goes all out for this proposal; he chooses the perfect location—the beach! He orders dozens upon dozens of perfect red roses for the occasion. He writes her name in the sand. He hires an orchestra to play her favorite song and orders a plane to write "Will you marry me?" in the sky. The woman shows up to this proposal site that is truly social media worthy—this proposal will go viral. Once the woman gets there, she sees the man who loves her on bended knee. She takes in the beautiful scene he has created just for her; his act of love moves her, but she does not respond to his proposal.

Instead, she takes it all in, takes tons of pictures so she can remember this moment, posts them online, smiles, and leaves. She was excited by the love of this man who had been pursuing her for years, and she took pictures because she wanted to capture this moment and reminisce on it in the days and years to come, but she stopped short of accepting his hand in marriage. She just wasn't ready for that type of commitment.

Does this example depict Christ and the cross? Not at all. This proposal scene is far too clean and romantic. The scene at the cross was bloody and painful. But this beach scene does demonstrate deep, extravagant love on behalf of one person and what it looks like for the other person to admire love but not respond to it. You can admire God and smile about what Jesus did on the cross but never respond to it. When you ***accept*** Salvation, you are responding to Jesus' offer; you are accepting a relationship with God through His Son. You are choosing to commit to God, and that initial commitment–that foundation–is needed before any work can be done in your spiritual home.

The good news is that Jesus went all out in His proposal, and He is just looking for a simple but heart-filled 'yes' from you. He makes it really easy. Romans 10:9-10 tells us, "If you declare with your mouth, 'Jesus is Lord,' and believe in your heart that God raised him from the dead, you will be saved. For it is with your heart that you believe and are justified, and it is with your mouth that you profess your faith and are saved."

Simple. Say, *"Jesus is Lord, and I believe that He died on the cross for me, and God raised him from the dead for me,"* and you are saved. This confession does not have to happen publicly. You can make this statement right now wherever you are sitting. You can make this statement in your bedroom, in your closet, or in your car. The key is that you believe what you are saying is true. The key is to accept the proposal, salvation, from your heart.

Jesus is Lord

Now that the foundation is laid and you have accepted Jesus into your heart, it is time for the framing. Let's take a second look at Romans 10:9 (NIV), which states the importance of declaring that "Jesus is Lord." This is a critical piece; let's spend time here. When you declare "Jesus is Lord," you set the framework for your spiritual home. "Jesus is Lord" is more than a statement; it is the construct, idea, framework, and model we use to build, create, and establish our spiritual home.

Many of us, me included, thought we could build a spiritual home, a temple for God that we fashioned. We thought we could live for God, but we would call the shots. Too many of us spend much of our walk with God negotiating the terms and conditions of our life because, at best, we believe we both are Lord of our life, we are equal with God, and we have equal say. Or, in the worst-case scenario, we believe we are greater than God, we are Lord, and we have the final say and rule over everything in our lives.

You may be thinking, *I would never believe that I am Lord of my life. I believe Jesus is Lord.* Pause. Let's break down lordship. In its most simple term, lordship means supreme power or rule. Someone or something that is a lord has power, authority, or influence. They are masters or rulers. Many lords (lowercase) exist throughout the world. Monarchies have lords throughout their kingdoms.

However, Romans 10:9 (CSB) tells us we are to declare that "Jesus is Lord." He is not just a lord; He is *the* Lord. He is the Lord of Lords. We are saying Jesus is the ultimate ruler; He has total power, authority, and influence in our lives. Paul wrote the book of Romans in Greek. The Greek word for Lord that he used when saying "Jesus is Lord" is *kyríos*, meaning master or principal, the chief, first in order.

First Corinthians 8:6 (CSB) says, "Yet for us there is one God, the Father. All things are from him, and we exist for him. And there is one Lord, Jesus Christ. All things are through him, and we exist through him." That means we are only here because of Jesus. We live our lives set apart for Jesus, so Jesus should have total authority, influence, and decision-making power in our lives.

Do not stop reading! This is the part where we usually walk away from our relationship with God through Jesus, or we choose to live a life that is 'believer lite'; a life where we believe in Jesus and accept Him as our Savior, but we only delegate specific authority to Him. He can influence how I raise my children, but I don't give him authority over my tongue and how I speak to people. He can decide what job I take, but He doesn't have decision-making power in my finances. And yes, I surrender my emotions to Jesus, but I don't allow Him to rule and regulate my thought life.

It is hard to wrap our minds around the framework of anyone–including Jesus–having that much power and say in our lives. But the truth is, that was the design all along. We weren't designed to be Lord of our life; we don't have enough knowledge, skill, or capacity to do so. It is not without cause that the scripture says, "For my thoughts are not your thoughts, neither are your ways, my ways, declares the Lord. As the heavens are higher than the earth, so are my ways higher than your ways and my thoughts than your thoughts" (Isaiah 55:8, NIV). For good reason, scripture tells us, "The foolishness of God is wiser than human wisdom, and the weakness of God is stronger than human strength" (1 Corinthians 1:25, NIV).

God is greater than you and me! God is wiser than us, more intelligent than us, more divine, more sovereign, more capable, all-knowing...the list goes on and on! That is why Jesus was always supposed to be Lord. Jesus gets His direction from God because God is His head, His Covering, His Lord. Then, by design, Jesus is the head, the Lord of man, the Lord of you and me (1 Corinthians 11:3).

The good news is that Jesus is an excellent Lord! Our situation would be bleak if Jesus were tyrannical, exercising power cruelly or arbitrarily. On the contrary, Jesus is a gracious and loving Lord. He comes into your spiritual home and makes improvements. Where there is confusion and calamity, He brings peace (Acts 10:36). He teaches you how to pursue peace (Hebrews 12:14). He dismisses worry and anxiety from your life (Matthew 6:34). He makes your home safe (Proverbs 18:10). Jesus shifts your life from just being busy to being productive (John 15:1).

The narrative that Jesus is not a good Lord is a false narrative crafted by the enemy, the devil, and this lie is believed by too many. The truth is, we are not fit to be Lord of our life. Now is the time; this is the moment in your life where you renounce your throne and make Jesus Lord. Yes, deferring to Jesus will be new and uncomfortable. But once you truly declare that Jesus is Lord, He will come into your physical home and, most importantly, your spiritual home and begin to make all things new. "Therefore, if anyone is in Christ, the new creation has come: The old has gone, the new is here" (2 Corinthians 5:17, ESV).

Will there be tension as you make Jesus Lord? Absolutely. Your flesh will still contend for the throne! Still, begin each day saying, *"Jesus is Lord. Jesus, have your way in my life today."* When you do this, you are calibrating yourself, ensuring your spiritual home is fashioned after Christ and living up to its original design.

Chapter Three

THE RESIDENT

"Do you not know that your bodies are temples of the Holy Spirit, who is in you, whom you have received from God? You are not your own." ~ 1 Corinthians 6:19 (NIV)

WE TALKED ABOUT THE foundation of your spiritual home and the necessary framing, but this home that God is building, this lifestyle you subscribe to, is not for your personal use. God is building your temple to be a suitable home for His Spirit, the Holy Spirit.

First Corinthians 6:19 (NIV) posed this question: "Do you know that your bodies are temples of the Holy Spirit?" That is not intended to be a rhetorical question. Did you know this? Your response may be yes, or it may be no. This is when I remind you or inform you for the first time that your body *is* intended to be a temple for the Holy Spirit. It feels like a contradiction given that in our flesh dwells no good thing (Romans 7:18), and our hearts are deceitful above all things and beyond cure (Jeremiah 17:9). But that's why

God purchased us with Jesus' blood so that we could be new (2 Corinthians 5:17). The Holy Spirit wants to dwell in your *new* temple.

In a physical house, the structures we build with concrete slabs and wood framing, anyone can inhabit the home. If an individual or a family has the necessary funds, they can purchase a home lot and build a house on it, or they can buy a house already built and on the market for sale. Once the house is purchased, the residents make it a home by adding their belongings, furniture, and design touches.

I say that to distinguish a physical home and a spiritual one. God purchased our spiritual homes, and they are being built with the express purpose of housing the Holy Spirit. No other spirit is welcome to dwell on the inside of us. As a matter of fact, other spirits, like the spirits of pride, envy, lust, perversion, malice, etc., are intruders in the home that God purchased and is continuing to build on.

We cannot glorify God without God's Spirit living inside us. The Holy Spirit is the one who reveals God to us and enables us to reflect God in the Earth. Think about it this way: You have your parents' DNA living inside you, producing the physical features the world sees (e.g., your hair, your smile, your height, your eyes... your everything). Your parents' DNA is woven into your physical makeup, determining what the world sees.

When God's Holy Spirit lives on the inside of you, God's person lives on the inside of you, so His spiritual DNA is what the world should see when they see you. We will park here momentarily and get grounded on the Holy Spirit. First and foremost, He is a person. God is a three-part being: God the Father, Jesus the Son, and the Holy Spirit. The Holy Spirit, like God, was here from the beginning. We first learn that God is a three-part being in Genesis 1:26 (NIV), when God said, "Let **us** make mankind in **our** image, in **our** likeness, so that they may rule over the fish in the sea and the birds in the sky, over the livestock and all the wild animals."

Using the words 'us' and 'our' was not an accident or use of the wrong pronoun. It is evidence that God acted in harmony with Jesus and the Holy Spirit when He created all things in the beginning. I give this historical context so you understand that the Holy Spirit is not new or separate from God. As a matter of fact, He was a part of the redemption strategy. God sent His Son to defeat sin, hell, and the grave once and for all and to restore God's relationship with His children. Before Jesus returned to heaven to be with the Father (God), He promised the Holy Spirit would come after Him.

When Jesus was speaking to His disciples about His departure, He said to them, "Do not leave Jerusalem, but wait for the gift my Father promised, which you have heard me speak about. For John baptized with water, but in a few days, you will be baptized with the Holy Spirit" (Acts 1:4-5, NIV). Jesus went on to say, "But you will receive power when the Holy Spirit comes on you; and you will be my witnesses in Jerusalem, and in all Judea and Samaria, and to the ends of the earth (Acts 1:8)."

The gift of the Holy Spirit was not just a promise for the disciples of that time period; the offer did not expire. We have the same promise and access to the Holy Spirit now. The Holy Spirit is the connective tissue between us and God. John 4:24 (NIV) says, "God is a spirit, and his worshippers must worship in the Spirit and in truth." We need God's Spirit to experience true worship and fellowship with God. Moreover, we need the Holy Spirit to lead and guide us into all Truth so we can be more like our God (John 16:13). We need the Holy Spirit to teach us the thoughts of God and the ways of God so we can glorify God with all of our being. And that is the point, right? You are reading this book because you want to move beyond knowing God from a distance. You are tired of performative religion, and you want to really see what God can do in and through you!

Well, it starts with the Holy Spirit. The road to being a powerful and productive believer begins with inviting God's Holy Spirit to live on the inside of you. He needs to take up residence in your spiritual home. If you have not extended this invitation to the Holy Spirit, you can do it now. Say this prayer: *I believe in my heart that Jesus is Lord and that God raised him from the dead; with that, I am saved. Now, I ask God's Holy Spirit to dwell on the inside of me, lead and guide me into all truth, and empower me in my walk with God through Jesus Christ.*

With that prayer, the Holy Spirit will now make His dwelling on the inside of you. You might be wondering: *How will I know that the Holy Spirit dwells on the inside of me? I cannot see Him; I do not feel Him.* It will be evident that God's Spirit, the Holy Spirit, is dwelling on the inside of you when you start to hear the voice of God in your innermost being. It is not your conscience; it is not 'vibes'; it is God's voice speaking to you. You will hear His voice compelling you to do things that align with God's character, like extending grace to the person who upset you or praying for the homeless person you just saw lying in the street.

When you open your Bible to read and study the scriptures, you will experience a new interest and understanding because God's Spirit is stirring up your passion and curiosity and bringing new revelation to God's word. When the Holy Spirit dwells inside, He will caution you against engaging in activities that will compromise your relationship with God. He will compel you to draw closer to God and admonish you to avoid people, places, or things that do not glorify God. The Holy Spirit will become active in your prayer life. He will give you words to pray to your Father (God), and He will also take it a step further and pray to the Father on your behalf (Romans 8:26). The Holy Spirit is delighted to dwell in your home; He strengthens the bond between you and God.

Unwelcome Residents

Your spiritual home was built for the Holy Spirit to dwell; anyone or anything else seeking to take up space in your home is an unwelcome resident. You have to be really clear on this because you cannot give others room or even rental options. The Holy Spirit does not want to cohabitate with anything that does not glorify God.

Galatians 2:20 reads, "I have been crucified with Christ, and **I no longer live,** but Christ lives in me. The life I now live in the body, I live by faith in the Son of God, who loved me and gave himself for me" (NIV) This scripture tells us who the first unwelcome resident is and that is ***ourselves***. You may be thinking, *wait, that doesn't make sense; how can I not live in my own body? How can I be excluded from the home that God is building in me?* Excellent questions. The scripture is not literally saying your physical man cannot be on the scene. As long as we are living, breathing humans on Earth, we are present in our bodies. However, the Holy Spirit, who is one with God and Jesus Christ, lives on the inside of our body. He is Lord, and He sets the standard for our home.

We are admonished in Galatians 2 that our fleshy behaviors should not take up room in the house God purchased and is building. Our flesh does not have authority in our home, nor do we give it a place to dictate our actions. When I say "flesh," I don't mean the physical skin you are wrapped in. Flesh is our human nature aligned with worldly passions and affirmed by sinful acts. Our flesh contradicts the Spirit of God (Galatians 5:17). Our fleshly nature has an identity of its own and very clear behaviors. "The acts of the flesh are obvious: sexual immorality, impurity, and debauchery (excessive indulgence in sensual pleasures); idolatry and witchcraft; hatred, discord, jealousy, fits of rage, selfish-ambition, dissensions, factions, and envy; drunkenness, orgies and the like" (Galatians 5:19-20, NIV).

The list above does not capture every act of the flesh, but as you can see, the acts of the flesh are extensive. It is also important to note that the acts of the flesh are not limited to sexual misdeeds; the list noted fits of rage, self-ambition, hatred, etc. We often limit fleshly or worldly behaviors to sexual impurity and promiscuity. The scripture was more inclusive than that; it spoke to many behaviors that tend to go unchecked in our lives. It is important to call out these fleshly behaviors because when they show up in your life, they should alert you there is an intruder in your home. This intruder is not the devil or one of his companions. This intruder was once in control; it had a key and full access to your home. This intruder is your flesh, your human nature, your personal desires. And even though you accepted Salvation, declared Jesus is Lord, and invited the Holy Spirit to dwell in your home, the flesh is always trying to regain entry.

What does that look like? The flesh does not physically knock on the door of your spiritual home or try to break a window in your new place. After all, there are no physical doors or windows to trespass. However, the flesh makes daily attempts to entice you into giving it a place to stay again. James 1:14-15 (NIV) says this: "But each person is tempted when they are dragged away by *their own* evil desire and enticed. Then, after desire has conceived, it gives birth to sin; and sin, when it is full-grown, gives birth to death."

The flesh is persistent and makes daily attempts to be a part of your life again. The flesh is crafty; it knows what you desire as an individual and customizes its call to your specific wants. Some acts of the flesh are general for all of us, and then there are other acts of the flesh that may be more pervasive in your life than in the life of your brother or sister, friend, or co-worker. We all have the propensity to be jealous, but jealousy is a more familiar resident to some than others. The same is true for fits of rage, drunkenness, hatred, etc. Most people experience these fleshly acts at some point in their lives, but these behaviors are more at home in some people than others.

This is true for a variety of reasons. Our upbringing can make you or me lean more towards some acts of flesh than others. Or perhaps you are more prone to specific fleshly acts like sexual immorality or jealousy because you entertained these residents more than you entertained others. I don't say this to point fingers at anyone but to bring awareness. You have to hold hands with God as He is building your spiritual home because, in the building process, God will reveal to you the fleshly behaviors that are more likely to try to take up space in your home.

So, we know that our fleshly desires and behaviors are unwelcome residents, but there are other intruders that were not birthed out of our human nature. These spirits came from our enemy, the devil, and their goal is to take full possession of our spiritual home. They do not want to stay for a day or a long weekend. Once they enter your home, they want to stay for a lifetime. These spirits will travel alone but prefer to travel in a pack. They want to regulate your every move and action. These spirits wreak havoc in your heart and mind; they work to destroy your relationships with people, and their ultimate goal is to create separation between you and God.

No, you are not reading a ghost story, and I am not trying to spook you. I do, however, need you to be well-informed about the activity that is taking place in the spirit realm and how the enemy sends spirits to invade your spiritual home. Let's go to Mark 1:21-28 (NIV) to learn more about these intruders:

> They went to Capernaum, and when the Sabbath came, Jesus went into the synagogue and began to teach. The people were amazed at his teaching because he taught them as one who had authority, not as the teachers of the law. Just then, a man in their synagogue who was possessed by an impure spirit cried out, 'What do you want with us, Jesus of Nazareth? Have you come

to destroy us? I know who you are-the Holy One of God!' 'Be Quiet!' Said Jesus sternly. 'Come out of him!' The impure spirit shook the man violently and came out of him with a shriek. The people were all so amazed that they asked each other, 'What is this? A new teaching and with authority! He even gives orders to impure spirits, and they obey him.' News about him (Jesus) spread quickly over the whole region of Galilee.

There is so much to unpack from this scriptural account in Mark. First, I want to point out that there was a man who was a part of the synagogue who had an impure spirit. That suggests that he regularly went to church service and fellowshipped with other synagogue members, but an impure spirit still possessed him. Why? Because impure or unclean spirits do not go away simply because you attend church service. It was not until the impure spirit was in the presence of Jesus, who has authority over every spirit, that the spirit had to submit to the Holy One and leave the man.

Jesus does not physically walk the Earth as a man anymore. But when we accept salvation through Jesus Christ and invite God's Holy Spirit to live inside us, we also have access to the same power and authority in Mark 1. We have the divine right to call on the name of Jesus and to tell impure spirits that they can no longer possess our homes. The term 'impure spirit' is a name that captures all of the spirits that come from the devil. However, these spirits have individual qualities and assignments and manifest themselves differently in different people. Some spirits are very boisterous and more obvious, while others are more subtle. At this point, you are probably thinking, *how do I know if I have an impure spirit? How can I distinguish between an act of my flesh and an unclean spirit? And what am I supposed to do with all of this information?*

God wants you to be informed about these unwelcome residents so you can seek Him for specific guidance, instruction, and protection. The reality is that we all have different intruders who are working against our spiritual household, but there is one God, and He has the authority to bring order to our spiritual homes. God knew when He took claim of us that our fleshly acts would not go quietly into the night. He also knew there would be impure spirits who would dig their heels in and seek to continue occupying territory in our hearts, minds, and spirits. In His supreme wisdom, God gave us a plan for keeping unwelcome occupants at bay and tools to use as we engage in day-to-day spiritual warfare.

God has a strategy for driving out demonic spirits (Luke 11:20-21). God will teach you how to cover your spiritual home daily with the armor of God (Ephesians 6:11-18). He will tell you to guard your heart because everything flows from it (Proverbs 4:23). He will teach you where to place your focus and attention each day so the flesh cannot cause disturbance in your spiritual home (Isaiah 26:3)

God recognizes that fleshly ways and spirits are working overtime to gain access to your spiritual home, which God has accounted for. God provides security and protection plans to keep you and your spiritual home safe and free from intruders.

Care For Your House

God's Holy Spirit is delighted to live in your spiritual home. He finds joy in taking up space in your residence and is the best tenant you will ever have living in your spiritual home. Now that you have God's Spirit living on the inside, you are responsible for maintaining a home worthy of the Holy Spirit's presence.

God's Spirit understands that you are an earthly dwelling wrapped in flesh, and you engage in spiritual warfare daily. That is why the Holy Spirit wants to occupy every square foot in your home and continue to enlarge His space. He wants to love on you and teach you so you can be spiritually mature and complete, not lacking anything (James 1:4). Meanwhile, your enemy, the devil, is seeking to reclaim the space that he previously owned in your life. He is constantly working to make you divert back to the person you were, the habits you loved, the worldview you lived by, etc.

Your job, and mine, is to care for our spiritual home so we can win the daily battle between our flesh and God's Spirit. Galatians 5: 16-17 (NIV) says it this way, "So I say, walk by the Spirit, and you will not gratify the desires of the flesh. For the flesh desires what is contrary to the Spirit, and the Spirit what is contrary to the flesh. They are in conflict with each other, so that you are not to do whatever you want."

This ongoing conflict between our flesh and God's spirit is spiritual warfare, and you and I are engaged in it daily. Before you read this book, you were enlisted in spiritual warfare; while reading this book, you are in combat, and after you read this book, the war will continue. Many of us lose sight of this fact; we let down our guard, and in doing so, the enemy gains territory in our spiritual home. He gets the primary bedroom, and God's Holy Spirit is cramped on the fold-out couch.

We must intentionally care for our spiritual home and maintain a steady diet of what God's Spirit craves. Every time we feed our Spirit, He gains more ground. When we walk by the Spirit and follow His lead, we give Him more space in our home. This is where most of us have a steep learning curve. We know very well what our flesh craves and are accustomed to giving it what it wants and needs. We are not, however, well-versed in what the Holy Spirit needs. That means we have something to learn. Ephesians 5:10 tells us we must "find out what pleases the Lord." We are not expected to know how to feed God's Spirit, which lives inside us; we must learn.

I am a mom, and I can recall when I found out I was pregnant with my first child. First, the fact that life can grow inside you is a crazy, miraculous phenomenon! That aside, as soon as I knew that there was a little life on the inside of me, I was eager to learn what I needed to do to care for this being who was taking up residence inside me. I wanted to know what *to do,* like take prenatal vitamins, eat nutritious meals, do light exercises, etc. I also wanted to know the things *not to do,* like consume caffeine, lift heavy items, be around cigarette smoke, etc.

I was invested in learning the 'dos and don'ts' of pregnancy because I was invested in the life living inside me and its development. I was willing to deny myself some of my regular pleasures or routines so I could protect what I was housing. I say this because you must develop that same level of care, protection, and 'want to' regarding God's Holy Spirit. I will level with you. It is easier to take that approach for a tangible baby, *your* baby, that is growing inside your womb. Still, the passion and the intention have to be there for God's Holy Spirit.

Now is the time to shift your mindset. Your body *is* the temple of God's Holy Spirit. You are not your own. You are called to glorify God with your being. You must choose to move to the rhythm of God's drum; you have to move differently now. Since we live by the Spirit, we must keep in step with the Spirit (Galatians 5:25). This is not a suggestion for believers in Jesus Christ; it is our responsibility.

Chapter Four

THE NEIGHBORHOOD

"He has rescued us from the domain of darkness and transferred us into the kingdom of the Son he loves." ~ Colossians 1:13 (NIV)

MY HUSBAND AND I built our home in Apopka, FL. As I shared earlier in the book, we purchased a lot, received a permit from the city, and began building our new home. We closed on our home in March of 2021. We were so excited when we signed our closing papers and received the key to our first home! Shortly after moving into our home, we received information in the mail about our Homeowner's Association (HOA). Yes, we purchased our home and were responsible for the monthly mortgage payments, utilities, lawn maintenance, and pest control. Still, we moved into a deed-restricted community managed by an HOA. The HOA outlines rules that regulate the neighborhood's appearance and how each person must maintain their property. Every homeowner pays due to the association and is expected to follow their guidelines.

For example, the HOA dictates the paint colors you can use when you want to repaint your home. The HOA also regulates how high you can let your grass grow, how green you must keep your grass, and they tell you what type of basketball hoop you can have in your yard and the hours of the day you can park your car on the side of the street. While some may feel the rules are unfair or excessive, my husband and I have grown to appreciate our deed-restricted community. The overarching guidelines for all homesites in our subdivision help ensure that everyone's grass is well-manicured, the streets are clear, and no one paints their home hot pink, thereby bringing down the property value of all the homes in the community, including ours.

Our spiritual homes also have an "HOA." No, there is not an association that collects quarterly dues and sends out enforcement letters if your sod is turning brown, but our spiritual home is subject to the rules of the Kingdom, God's Kingdom. Let's go back to the opening verse for this chapter, which reads, "He (God) has rescued us from the domain of darkness and transferred us into the kingdom of the Son he loves" (Colossians 1:13, NIV).

We live in this world, but when Jesus is Lord of our life, we are under His jurisdiction, surrender to His power, respect His authority, and submit to the rules of God's Kingdom. When you accepted Salvation, you declared with your mouth, "Jesus is Lord." Every Lord has a Kingdom, a realm, a principality, a territory, a domain. We need to take a moment and really unpack what a kingdom is so we understand the governance of our spiritual home.

I deeply studied the Holy Bible to learn more about God's Kingdom. I own Tony Evan's Study Bible and want to ensure I give credit to Pastor and Author Tony Evans. I cherish the study Bible he penned and all of the teachings therein. Specifically, Tony Evans broke down God's Kingdom and His comprehensive rule in a way that I want to lift directly from his Bible commentary and share with you. Tony Evans explained the Kingdom of God is His rule, plan, and program. It is all-embracing, covering everything in the universe. Therefore, we can define the Kingdom as God's comprehensive rule over all creation. Tony Evans said the Kingdom agenda may be defined as the visible manifestation of the comprehensive rule of God over every area of your life. The Greek word that Scripture uses for "kingdom" is *basileia*. It means "a rule" or "authority," including the concept of power. Every kingdom has a king or ruler. Every king or ruler has subjects.

In addition, a kingdom includes a realm, a domain over which the king rules. A kingdom has regulations or guidelines that govern the relationship between the ruler and the subjects. These are necessary so that the subjects know they are doing what the ruler wants done. In summary, Tony Evans said God's Kingdom includes all of the elements of a traditional kingdom. He is the absolute ruler of His domain, which encompasses all creation. Likewise, His authority is total. Everything God rules, He runs. And He has made His guidelines known in His Word (*Tony Evans Study Bible*, p.1414, 2019).

You must understand and become comfortable with God's Kingdom governing your spiritual home. Some people do not wish to build or buy homes in deed-restricted communities because they do not want a person or an association to rule over and dictate what they can do with their homes on their property. But remember, God purchased you; you are not your own, and therefore, your spiritual home falls under his domain.

You have relationship with God through Jesus, and as I said earlier in the book, Jesus is an awesome Lord! He is righteous, Holy, thoughtful, wise, and more capable of ruling your home than you are. To truly glorify God with your body and your entire being, you must become a subject of the Kingdom and adopt God's guidelines and principles in your spiritual home. Pleasing the King and patterning your life after Him has to mean more than pleasing people. The Apostle Paul says it this way, "Am I now trying to win the approval of human beings, or of God? Or am I trying to please people?

If I were still trying to please people, I would not be a servant of Christ" (Galatians 1:10, NIV).

Pleasing God has to mean more than pleasing yourself. You cannot be a Kingdom resident while living according to your own rules and standards. You have to forfeit your own wants, desires, and plans for your life to truly glorify God with your entire being.

You may be thinking one of two things at this point: *I don't think I am up for this, submitting myself to God's rules, and* two, *I want to live according to God's standards, but I don't even know what He expects from me.* To the first thought, I say this: do not be stiff-necked, stubborn, deliberate, or fixed in the mentality that God cannot tell you what to do. Have you noticed that we usually become most uncomfortable and unwilling to comply when *God* sets the standard, the rule? I will say it more plainly: when your employer tells you to wear a specific uniform or attire, you wear it. If your child's sports team says they have a game at 8 AM on a Sunday and you must be there, you arrive as asked. When your favorite music artist or playwright has a show that will be in town, they set the price of the tickets, and you pay for them. When your Greek fraternity or sorority sets bylaws for membership, you follow them. However, when God our Father, the Creator of the universe, the one who knit us together in our mother's womb, the One who loved us and sent His Son to die for us, the Great King... when He wants to establish His order in our life we balk at Him and become inflamed by the mere suggestion that God would want to control our lives.

We get irritated and infuriated and question the audacity of God as if He is not competent, capable, or worthy to regulate every area of our lives. The truth is that God has the right and authority, and He is the most qualified to manage our lives. Psalm 139:1-6 (NIV) says, "You have searched me, Lord, and you know me. You know when I sit down and when I rise; you perceive my thoughts from afar. You discern my going out and my lying down; you are familiar with all my ways. Before a word is on my tongue you, Lord, know it completely. You hem me in behind and before, and you lay your hand upon me. Such knowledge is too wonderful for me, too lofty for me to attain."

Why wouldn't you want God to have absolute rule and control in your life when He is the only one who knows you completely, and who has the wisdom and power to hem you in and keep you? We give control to lesser things and people every day. However, we hesitate to give absolute control to God who is wise and whose power is vast (Job 9:4). God who is holy and great (Psalms 77:13). God who has your best interest at heart at all times; a God who thinks thoughts of peace and not evil as it pertains to you (Jeremiah 29:11). A God who loves you immensely and deeply (Ephesians 2:4). Why would you deny this God, your God, absolute rule and reign in your home? Why would you refuse to let Him establish His Kingdom standard in your home?

To those who are thinking, *I want to live according to God's standards, but I don't even know what He expects from me.* You learn about God's standard in His written Word, the Holy Bible. My husband and I received a booklet detailing our neighborhood's guidelines and regulations, and we were careful to read every detail and expectation because we wanted to be in compliance and keep our community beautiful. When you want to please God and live according to His Kingdom, you will be intentional about reading His word. You will read more about the necessity of Bible study in the coming chapters, but for now, know God's standard is revealed in the Holy Bible.

Unlike my husband and I reading our HOA booklet, reading God's Word is not a matter of compliance. However, those who want to find out what pleases the Lord and His Kingdom agenda seek God in His written Word. The book of Ephesians 5:10 (NIV) instructs us by saying, "And find out what pleases the Lord." When you are diligent about reading your Bible, you are demonstrating you want to get to know more about God. You are not searching the scriptures for God's directives, His list of "dos and don'ts." When you dive into His Word, you seek Him out. Once you learn more about God and our Savior, Jesus Christ, you will also learn more about the realm of the Kingdom, Kingdom mentality, Kingdom blessings, and, yes, Kingdom expectations. God's Word is His Truth. His Truth sanctifies us; it sets us apart for God's use (John 17:17). You read it earlier, and you will hear it repeated throughout this book—you *are not your own* (1 Corinthians 6:19). With that understanding, you do not get to establish the rules for your life because you are not lord, you are not ruler.

Giving God absolute control of your home may feel unsettling, uncomfortable, or unnerving. You may feel uncertain about letting Him call all the shots, but letting God's Kingdom have comprehensive, full-scope, complete rule over your life is the only way that He can produce a life in you that will glorify Him. For too long, we have been trying to bear the image of God and produce His fruit while still maintaining our autonomy and our ability to make decisions on our own and dictate our direction. Today is the day to surrender control to Him. Your home needs God's rule.

Chapter Five

THE FURNISHINGS

"Since, then, you have been raised with
Christ, set your hearts on things above,
where Christ is seated at the right hand of
God. Set your minds on things above, not
earthly things." ~ Colossians 3:1-2 (NIV)

WE FINISHED BUILDING OUR home at the beginning of March 2021, and we closed at the end of that month. Once the closing papers were signed, we, the residents, were excited and ready to move into our new home! With our new key in hand, we opened the front door, took in the fresh paint smell, and walked into each newly carpeted room in awe! We were in awe of God and how He blessed us, and we were so grateful we could now call this beautiful structure home. The only thing missing at that point was the furnishings.

We stayed in our previous rental for the first few nights after closing day because we did not have any furniture in our new home. Furniture is necessary if you want something to sit on as you eat a meal or if you want something to sleep on at night. Your furniture clothes your new home; it is a practical need, but it also gives your home character.

Your spiritual home also needs furnishings and character. The furniture in this home is not a table, chairs, sofa, or bed. No, this furniture is not tangible; it is spiritual. When envisioning the items that will furnish your spiritual home, you must take a page from Colossians 3 and set your heart on things above, not earthly things.

Colossians 3:12-14 (NIV) gives us precise instructions on the items that need to adorn our spiritual home, "Therefore, as God's chosen people, holy and dearly loved, clothe yourselves with compassion, kindness, humility, gentleness, and patience. Bear with each other and forgive one another if any of you has a grievance against someone. Forgive as the Lord forgave you. And over all these virtues put on love, which binds them all together in perfect unity."

These virtues make our home beautiful and are necessary as we seek to glorify God with our entire being. Note that this scripture addresses God's chosen people, His holy (set apart) and dearly loved people. God is specifically talking to the children that He purchased with His Son's blood, those who accepted Salvation, and those who now want to glorify God with their lives; He is talking to you and me. I call that out because you and I are surrounded by people every day who are not setting their hearts and minds on things above, and they will choose to furnish their lives with all kinds of things.

However, *we* must make space in our lives for virtues like compassion, kindness, and gentleness. You may be thinking, *I know people who don't know God, and they are nice people. They demonstrate compassion and kindness.* That is a fact. I do not want to mess up anyone's theology, but there are people who do not walk with God and are really nice, good people. They may opt into some of these biblical virtues even if they do not choose to have a relationship with God through Jesus Christ.

These furnishings are not an option for you and me, who are on a mission to glorify God with our entire being. Moreover, the Holy Spirit living on the inside of us enables us to consistently walk out these virtues with God's grace. In doing so, we amplify God, and He gets the glory.

Compassion

Compassion, by definition, is sympathetic pity and concern for the sufferings or misfortunes of others. Words synonymous with compassion are understanding, care, and empathy. Let's examine this virtue in more detail.

There is a debate among theologians (experts in the study of God) about who wrote the book of Colossians, where we find this list of virtues, the furnishings for our spiritual home. However, most theologians agree the Apostle Paul penned this letter to the Colossian church and wrote it to the people of Colossae in Greek.

With that context in mind, let's look at the word compassion in Greek. One Greek word for compassion is *oiktirmós*, which means to show pity or mercy. Another Greek word for compassion is *splagxnízomai,* meaning the stirring of the inward parts, literally the twisting of intestines. "It is a gut-wrenching, emotional response that is so strong that we are physically moved to action (Biblestudytools.com)."

Wow! Looking at the word compassion in Greek gives a whole new meaning to this virtue. It is more profound than empathizing with a person and feeling their pain. When you have compassion for someone, it disrupts you from the inside, jolts you, and moves you to action. You feel obligated to sincerely pray for the person or situation at hand. You have a healthy unrest that will not allow you to turn away or keep scrolling down your social media feed. When you see someone in need, you feel like it is your responsibility to help.

No, you are not Jesus. He saves, you don't. Still, you should feel an internal pull, a pressing to help when you see someone in need. When Jesus walked this Earth as a man, He experienced hunger, grew tired, and felt weak at times, but Jesus always pushed past his own circumstances to show compassion to others. We see this play out in Matthew 14:13 (NIV), "When Jesus landed and saw a large crowd, he had compassion on them and healed their sick." Moments before Jesus saw the large crowd and had compassion on them, He learned John the Baptist (his cousin) was beheaded.

Jesus was grieving the loss of His loved one, but when He saw the large crowd that gathered to see Him and that needed Him, He was stirred from the inside, moved to heal the sick, and ultimately, God received the glory. How does all of this apply to you? I am glad you asked. When we purpose in our hearts to glorify God with our being, we pattern ourselves after Jesus, who exercised compassion daily.

We aim to be more and more like Jesus every day, and because He was called to be compassionate, we have that same call. This is why we must furnish our spiritual home with compassion. It may not be the prettiest piece of furniture to you. In actuality, compassion can be quite unattractive from a human perspective. It is difficult and often a sacrifice to go beyond your situation, needs, and schedule to extend God's love to someone or to give from your household resources. But genuine compassion stretches you! It requires action on your part. It goes beyond just saying you will pray for someone; compassion wakes you up in the middle of the night to actually pray for that person.

Compassion doesn't passively sit by and see someone in pain; it moves you to stop what you are doing and lend your ear and a hug to someone hurting. Compassion will move you to give financial resources to someone when you may feel you don't have enough resources for yourself. Still, you do it because God is using you to bless someone in that moment. When you commit to living a life of compassion and being a vessel that God can use to lift others up and point them to God, you glorify God in your being.

Isn't that the point? Isn't that why you are so many pages into this book? You want God to make a spiritual home in you, and you want to glorify God with your life. Ensuring that compassion is present in your home makes it attractive to others; it will draw onlookers as they see you extend yourself in ways that seem uncommon and sometimes unreasonable. Your family will notice as you empathize with their hurt and pray with them and for them. Co-workers will be impressed by your heart for people while working for a company that focuses only on business results, performance metrics, and profit. The compassion you show day in, and day out will prove that God's Spirit is living on the inside of you, and it will introduce others to God. Thereby, God gets the glory.

Glorifying God is not about yelling from the rooftops, "God is real!" You gain more traction with people, and God gets more glory from your life by the fruit you produce and the way you exercise deep compassion for those around you. Compassionate living is one of the best ways to reflect God on the earth.

Kindness

Kindness, by definition, is the quality of being friendly, generous, and considerate. The Greek word for kindness is chréstotés. Chréstotés means goodness, excellence, uprightness; it is derived from the Greek word chrēstos which means to be useful, profitable.

Kindness is one of the most valuable pieces of furniture in our spiritual home. What if God went through all the work of sacrificing His Son for our sins, redeeming us from sin and death, making us alive in Jesus Christ, sending his Holy Spirit to inhabit our home so we can reflect Jesus in the Earth, and then we walk into the world and do not extend kindness to the people we engage with every day? That would be an epic failure on our part because Jesus was kind; kindness is one of His most well-known character traits.

There are many examples of kindness in the Bible. Let us go to John 8 when the Pharisees (staunch religious leaders) caught a woman in the act of adultery and tried to make a spectacle of her. Jesus was in the middle of teaching a group in the temple courts, and the Pharisees brought this adulterous woman to Jesus, expecting Jesus to berate her, hurl accusations at her, shame her, and ultimately stone her for her sinful act. Instead, Jesus demonstrated kindness and gentleness. He wrote on the ground words that, to this day, are not known or documented. After writing in the ground, Jesus said to the Pharisees, "Let any one of you who is without sin be the first to throw a stone at her (John 8:7, NIV)." The woman's accusers left the scene, and the woman was left with Jesus. He said to her, "Woman, where are they? Has no one condemned you?" "No one, sir," she said. "Then neither do I condemn you," Jesus declared. "Go now and leave your life of sin" (John 8:10-11, NIV).

This is just one example of Jesus' kindness; He showed deep consideration for this woman who was in a very difficult moment in her life, and He extended gentleness and care for her in the midst of people seeking to belittle and dispirit her. This is kindness on a grand stage, but Jesus also showed kindness to children; He welcomed them into His presence and laid hands on them (Mark 10:13-15). He was a huge advocate of being kind to *everyone*, even those who mistreat us. He instructs us to "do good to those who hate you" (Luke 6:27, NIV).

People will know that we are in relationship with a kind Jesus and that we have knowledge about Him not because we say it but because we show it. Second Corinthians 2:14-15 (NIV) states, "But thanks be to God, who always leads us as captives in Christ's triumphal procession and **uses us to spread the aroma of the knowledge of him everywhere** (emphasis added). For we are to God the pleasing aroma of Christ among those who are being saved and those who are perishing."

Kindness is a sweet fragrance that attracts others to you, which points others to God, and thereby, God gets the glory out of your life. This may seem like elementary teaching to some of you reading this book, but I cannot stress enough how important it is that we are kind to others. Kindness brings God's fragrance and light into sour and dark places. We are living in times where people desperately need gentleness and true friendliness, not artificial "likes" and "loves." People need to feel the warmth of your smile and hear your genuine question "How are you doing today?" We take it a step further in kindness when we actually pause to listen to their response to this question and provide encouragement and comfort when they are having a hard day or moment. The world needs to hear your laughter and experience your kind manners as you hold the door for the elderly person behind you or allow someone to have the right of way in traffic. Simple acts of kindness are missing in our daily interactions, and the absence of these acts contributes to the coldness and callousness of the human heart and soul. In short, be kind.

Humility

The Greek word for humility is tapeinophrosynē, which means lowliness of mind, making oneself low or close to the ground. Humility is often misunderstood, and, particularly in religious settings, the teaching on humility is inaccurate. Some believers in Jesus Christ have interpreted humility to mean shrinking one's voice, dressing modestly, not being boisterous, and, in some regards, being a human doormat. Some of this thinking is accurate, but some is not. Let's unpack it.

We are instructed in 1 Peter 5:6 (NIV) to "Humble yourselves, therefore, under God's mighty hand, that he may lift you up in due time." The first act of humility is to humble ourselves before God. If we are not humbled, yielded, and low to the ground before God, any other acts of humility will be false; we will be posturing—just playing the part. Once we humbly submit to God (our vertical relationship), then we can exercise humility across our horizontal relationships.

The scriptures give clear guidance on how to live a life of humility. Philippians 2:3-4 (NIV) tells us, "Do nothing out of selfish ambition or vain conceit. Rather in humility, value others above yourselves, not looking to your own interests but each of you to the interest of others." When you do as Philippians 2 directs, you are making yourself low to the ground. It is not about having low self-esteem or allowing yourself to be a doormat; it is ensuring that in your spiritual home, you roll out the red carpet for others; you do not have a me-first mentality.

We are encouraged in Ephesians 4:2 (NIV) to "Be completely humble and gentle; be patient, bearing with one another in love." We glorify God with our being when we humble ourselves and bear with others. What does that look like? Suppose there is a disagreement or confusion in your relationship. In that case, it is you listening to understand what the other person is experiencing, leaving your 'high horse,' and meeting them where they are. It is letting the gentleness of God and His love that permeates you overrule your need to be right. It looks like lowering your defenses and opening your heart and mind to understand the needs of others. It looks like putting yourself low to the ground by pursuing peace, making every effort to live in peace with everyone, and to be holy (1 Peter 3:11; Hebrews 12:14).

Furnishing your spiritual home with humility can feel like you are clothing yourself in weakness, but that could not be further from the truth. It takes an *immense* amount of strength to walk in humility. As a woman, particularly a Black woman, I have not always had a positive relationship with humility. Disclaimer: I am not here to make a bold or blanket statement for all Black women. However, being a Black woman my entire life, I feel comfortable speaking from my personal reference point. Black women have so many obstacles to traverse personally and professionally, and often, these obstacles strengthen you and sharpen your skills, but they can also harden you. You can develop a "show no weakness, take no prisoners" mentality. Much of this mantra develops from the fact that, as Black women, we have to show up in settings and work twice as hard, be overly prepared, produce five times more results, etc.

I do not share this to go on a tangent or to solicit sympathy for the Black woman. I share this because it can be especially challenging to demonstrate humility, go low, and continually consider others above yourself when there is no reciprocity; others do not readily or consistently exercise humility. This goes back to my first point about humbling yourself before God first. When we surrender our thoughts, ideals, and emotions to God first, He (with the Holy Spirit living inside us) enables us to exercise humility with others. God gives us the strength and courage to be humble, and we don't need others to consider us for us to consider them. When we live a life of humility, we demonstrate that God is living on the inside of us, and He gets the glory out of our lives.

Gentleness

The Greek word for gentleness is prautés. It speaks to mildness of disposition, gentleness of spirit, meekness. Gentleness and kindness are furniture pieces that go hand in hand in your spiritual home, but one distinguishing feature is this attribute: mildness of disposition. Gentleness is more than performing kind or gentle acts. It is about your internal disposition, your temperament.

I think we can all recall a time when we extended kindness or were gentle with someone, but on the inside, every bell, whistle, and heated fire alarm was going off! We overrode our fleshly response and were kind in turn, but on the inside, we were experiencing a fit of rage; we were casting judgment or being overly critical of the person or situation. As God is building our spiritual home, He is investing in furniture like gentleness because He is not just interested in how we show up to the world and those around us; he is interested in our spiritual disposition and what is happening inside of us.

You may wonder: *Do I get credit for being kind and gentle even though my inner disposition did not align with my outward actions?* The answer is, God is first interested in what happens inside your spiritual home. Once you clothe yourself with gentleness from the inside, the outside behaviors will follow, and there will be less internal tension and friction because the behavior will come more naturally.

When we talk about glorifying God with our being, we have to remember that God is interested and invested in our being. Unlike the Pharisees of the Bible days and the performative Christians and religious folks of today, God is not impressed when we feign godliness and strive to get credit for doing things that we think will please God. As a matter of fact, Jesus said in Matthew 23:25-26 (NIV), "Woe to you, teachers of the law and Pharisees, you hypocrites! You clean the outside of the cup and dish, but inside, they are full of greed and self-indulgence. Blind Pharisee! First, clean the inside of the cup and dish, and then the outside will also be cleaned."

In other words, let God work on the inside of your spiritual home; let him rehab your internal disposition. Bring in furniture pieces like gentleness to take up space on the inside of you so your gentle and kind acts [that you show the world] merely reflect your internal condition.

Patience

The Greek word for patience is hupomoné, which means the ability to stand under, especially when there is a heavy load of trial, persecution, adversity, trouble, or pain. Hupomoné is constancy and consistency. Reading this

Greek definition should be eye-opening and transformative; it should shift your thinking on the word patience.

Patience is not just your ability to wait an extra five minutes in line because the coffee shop is behind on making orders. Patience is much deeper than your ability to repeat the same direction to your child for the fifth time today. Patience is a crucial furniture piece in our spiritual homes, and it cannot be executed correctly in our lives without the empowering of God's Holy Spirit.

When we dig deep into the well of God's Holy Spirit and allow Him to give us patience, that is how we have staying power in our walk with Jesus Christ; that is how we keep consistency in our relationship with God even in the face of hard times (Romans 12:12). Patience spurs us to carry the load with our brothers and sisters, friends, and co-workers because we draw on God's strength. It allows us to bear with others in times of adversity, trouble, and pain.

Patience is a virtue that exemplifies God living on the inside of us. It shows strength and resilience that will compel others to connect with God so they can have that same power and resiliency in their own lives. This again points others to God, and He gets the glory.

Forgiveness

The God-virtues that we need for our spiritual home include forgiveness. Let's go back to Colossians 3:13 (NIV), "Bear with each other and forgive one another if any of you has a grievance against someone. Forgive as the Lord forgave you."

The idea of forgiving someone who has wronged you (intentionally or unintentionally) can be a hard pill for most of us to swallow. In Matthew 18, we see Jesus' first disciples had questions on the topic of forgiveness. Peter asked, "Lord how many times shall I forgive my brother or sister who sins against me? Up to seven times?" Jesus answered, "I tell you, not seven times, but seventy-seven times (Matthew 18:21-22, NIV)." I read that conversation between Jesus and His disciples and thought: *Man, I don't know if I can live up to that standard of forgiveness.*

But God gave me clarity on forgiveness, and He wants to give you clarity on forgiveness, too. First, you probably already know that forgiveness is not for the sake of another person but for you. God is invested in *your* spiritual home, which houses His Holy Spirit. With that, God understands you need forgiveness so you can walk in peace. Proverbs 19:11 (NIV) states, "A person's wisdom yields patience; it is to one's glory to overlook an offense." That scripture couples well with Hebrews 12:15 (NIV), which reads, "See to it that no one falls short of the grace of God and that no bitter root grows up to cause trouble and defile many."

It is wise to forgive offenses quickly; it is to your glory (your benefit) to do so because if you do not, you leave room for a root of bitterness to grow in your spiritual home. That bitterness defiles your home. How does it defile your home? One, it weakens your prayer life (Mark 11:25; Matthew 6:15). Two, bitterness is a bedfellow with malice. When malice is in your home, it gives space to fleshly acts, and the flesh never acts in accordance with God's will or His character. It is for good reason that Colossians 3:7-8 (NIV) says, "You used to walk in these ways, in the life you once lived. **But now** you must rid yourself of all such things as these: anger, rage, **malice**, slander, and filthy language from your lips." You do not want to give way to these expressions of the flesh.

When you forgive, you deny access to anger, rage, and malice in your spiritual home and (you) give God access and permission to heal your heart. "The Lord is close to the brokenhearted and saves those who are crushed in spirit" (Psalm 34:18, NIV). When you forgive, you leave room for God to address the situation or your offender: "It is mine to avenge; I will repay, says the Lord" (Romans 12:19, NIV).

If you need another reason to forgive, know that when you do not forgive, you grieve God's Holy Spirit. When bitterness takes root in your spiritual home, it lends itself to rage, anger, malice, etc., making it uncomfortable and uninhabitable for God's Spirit. Why? Because these traits directly contradict the traits of God, the fruits of the Spirit. "The fruit of the Spirit is love, joy, peace, forbearance, kindness, goodness, faithfulness, gentleness, and self-control" (Galatians 5:22-23, NIV). Unforgiveness creates a root of bitterness, and the fruit from a bitter tree conflicts with the fruits of the Spirit and creates disharmony.

This is why Ephesians 4:30-32 (NIV) says, "And do not grieve the Holy Spirit of God, with whom you were sealed for the day of redemption. **Get rid of all bitterness**, rage and anger, brawling and slander, along with every form of malice. Be kind and compassionate to one another, **forgiving each other**, just as in Christ God forgave you."

We are spending time on forgiveness because it is a really big deal. If you are anything like me, carrying out forgiveness has been a pain point in your walk with God or in your life in general. Here is something I learned as I was writing this book: Forgiveness is difficult, in part, because we try to operate in forgiveness before we have furnished our spiritual home with the previous virtues we discussed: compassion, kindness, humility, patience, and gentleness.

If we haven't put on compassion in our spiritual home, we haven't allowed God's Holy Spirit to stir our inward parts, to move us to help other people (whether they deserve it or not). Without compassion, we are likely going to struggle with forgiveness. Moreover, forgiveness will be a perpetual challenge if we haven't humbled ourselves before God, made ourselves low to the ground, and considered others before ourselves. Even more, if we have not let patience do its work on the inside of our spiritual home so we can bear with others in hard times, endure pain, and remain consistent under pressure, we will wrestle with forgiveness and lose on most occasions.

If you are having a hard time extending forgiveness to someone or even to yourself, it could be for various reasons. The hurt may be too deep, or the shame may be too piercing. But I encourage you to sit with God on where your struggle lies with forgiveness. Understand that forgiveness begins as a choice, and you have to choose to forgive. However, if you are having difficulty making that choice and walking out forgiveness, it may be a sign that you need to embrace more compassion, kindness, or even humility. Forgiving people, including yourself, is necessary for a healthy relationship with God. Extending forgiveness is also crucial for every believer who wants to glorify God with their being. God is forgiving, and we take our cues from Him.

Love

Love ties all of these furnishings (virtues) together in perfect unity (Colossians 3:14). God *is* love. First John 4:7 (NIV) states, "Dear friends, let us love one another, for love comes from God. Everyone who loves has been born of God and knows God. Whoever does not love does not know God because God is love."

The kind of love that John is talking about gets lost in translation for most of us because we use the word "love" to express our appreciation for our favorite meal. We also "love" sports teams and walks on the beach. However, this love is deeper, more meaningful, and in a separate class of its own—it is *agape* love.

Agape love is God's standard of love; it is the highest kind of love. You *will* yourself to love in this manner and deliberately choose to demonstrate this type of love because it is uncommon and unnatural. You need God's Holy Spirit living on the inside of you to enable you to love in this fashion. First

Corinthians 13:4-7 (NIV) tells us about agape love: "Love is patient, love is kind. It does not envy; it does not boast it is not proud. It does not dishonor others, it is not self-seeking, it is not easily angered, it keeps no record of wrongs. Love does not delight in evil but rejoices with the truth. It always protects, always trusts, always hopes, always perseveres."

We must furnish our spiritual home with God's standard of love because that is how we *truly* glorify God with our being. Jesus told his disciples, "By this everyone will know that you are my disciples if you love one another (John 13:35, NIV)."

God wrote your life story, and agape love is His signature. When you love as God loves, you reveal to the world who God is, and your life testifies that He is the author and finisher of your faith (Hebrews 12:2). Everything you have read up until this moment is vital information. It will help you glorify God, but the call to love is the most significant call to action. Your spiritual home needs to be filled with God's love to the point of overflowing. You need to receive the love that God is pouring out to you, bask in it, and let it overflow into your interactions with people. God's love is abundant and intended to be reproduced over and over in our lives because we receive His love in such abundance. We can generously love others because God first loved us (1 John 4:19).

Chapter Six

A HOUSE OF WORSHIP

"God is spirit, and his worshippers must worship in the Spirit and in truth" ~ *John 4:24* (NIV)

WHEN WE WERE LOOKING for a home for our family, my husband and I stalked developer websites looking for information on their up-and-coming homesites, and we anxiously waited for them to erect model homes in new-build communities so we could tour the model homes and see if that subdivision would be right for our family. As we toured model homes, we walked through the main living spaces and bedrooms and envisioned our family living there. Much like Goldilocks and the Three Bears narrative, we would say, *"This room would be great for the kids,* or *this kitchen feels too cramped for our family,"* or, *"This would be a great space for the Christmas tree when December rolls around."* Before we ever signed a purchase agreement, we were making plans for how our family would stretch out in the new space and what activities we would enjoy.

God is also proactive and a planner. Before you ever thought about your spiritual home, He made plans for the Holy Spirit to live on the inside of you, and He made plans for the types of activities that would take place in your spiritual home. One activity God planned is worship. God designed your spiritual home to be a house of worship. Yes, you physically go to the house of worship and fellowship at your local church (Hebrews 10:25). However, God intends for *you* to *be* a house of worship.

You might be thinking, *I am not a singer. I don't play an instrument. How can I be a house of worship?* Worship is so much more than the slow song sung during church service. Worship is an expression of reverence (deep respect), adoration(love), and devotion to something. We worship God through songs that we sing in church service; we express our love and respect for Him. However, that is only one form of worship and one location where we worship.

Our spiritual homes should be houses of worship; there should be ongoing worship service inside our temple. Every day we open our eyes on this Earth we should express our reverence and adoration for God. John 4:24 tells us that worshipping God is a spiritual act. That means we need God's Spirit living inside us to truly connect with God intimately.

Before we get too far into the conversation on worship, I need to distinguish between worship and praise. Praise is rejoicing or thanking God for who He is or what He has done or will do in your life. Anyone can praise God, and as a matter of fact, the scripture instructs *everything* to praise the Lord. "Let everything that has breath praise the Lord" (Psalm 150:6, NIV). Worship, however, requires intimacy with God through His Spirit.

This is why worship at the physical church and in our spiritual homes can sometimes be more of a struggle. We must humble ourselves to bow at the throne of God and express our deepest regard, respect, love, and devotion to Him. Worship requires sacrifice, and we are the sacrificial offering. We have to surrender our pride, our emotions, our will, our priorities—ourselves in order to *truly* worship God. This is why Romans 12:1 (NIV) tells us, "Therefore, I urge you, brothers, and sisters, in view of God's mercy, to offer your bodies as a living sacrifice, holy and pleasing to God-this is your true and proper worship."

The truth is we cannot worship God and ourselves or our ideals simultaneously. We have to surrender to His Spirit and bow to His deity in order to truly worship Him. There are many forms of worship to God, but there is only one passageway to worship: through the Spirit.

In case you didn't know, worshipping God has always been the objective for those who believe in Him. Let's take a trip back to Egypt around 1446 BC. You are likely familiar with the story of Moses and the Israelites, but if you are not, here is the short story: The Israelites (God's Chosen People) were in bondage in Egypt for 430 years (Exodus 12:40). During these generations of slavery, the Israelites assimilated to Egyptian culture to include, eating their food, following their practices, and worshipping their gods.

Moses was chosen and charged by God to lead the Israelites out of the bondage in Egypt. Moses received this specific instruction from God, "Go to Pharaoh (the ruler of Egypt) and tell him: This is what the Lord says: Let my people go, **so that they may worship me** (Exodus 8:1)." The purpose of freedom was so God's people could freely worship *their* God, the true and living and God (Jeremiah 10:10).

Today, we live to carry out that same purpose in our spiritual homes; we live to worship God. This is why worship is so much more than a lullaby that we sing to God; it is deeper than a second selection on a song list. We worship God with our being; God's Spirit, who resides inside us, propels our worship. He reveals God's glory to us from the inside, which results in an external expression of reverence and adoration.

Worship Through Prayer

We can also express reverence and adoration to God when we pray. When we move beyond the "God will (you) please…" prayers and push past the "I need you to help me…" petitions, we can enter a place of worship when we talk to God. When we open our mouths and boast about the majesty and might of God, and when we use our lips to speak about the goodness of God and His sovereignty, we are worshipping Him. When we take the focus off of ourselves, our needs, and our immediate surroundings, and instead, we yield the floor to God and lock in on His greatness, we are worshipping. When we stand in awe of God and declare His holiness and righteousness in contrast to our humanity and our weakness, we are worshipping. When we tell Him how beautiful He is, how faithful He is, and how grateful we are that He is our God, we are worshipping. Without a note being played on a keyboard or a song being sung by a worship leader, we are worshipping. We are bowing at God's throne, lifting Him up because He is great, and magnifying Him in our spiritual homes.

Worship Through Giving

When we return the tithe (the first tenth of our income) to God and when we give an offering, we also worship God. Anytime money leaves our hands or bank accounts, it can easily feel like a transaction. However, when you return to God the tithe as he instructed (Malachi 3:10) and bring an offering (Psalms 96:8), you are not just transacting; you are worshipping. In the same manner, you use your lips to express deep respect, love, and devotion to God; you do the same thing with your finances. You are demonstrating your deep love and devotion to God and honoring Him with your treasure.

Matthew 6:21 clearly tells us that where your treasure is, your heart will also be there. Matthew 6:24 (NIV) continued, "No one can serve two masters. Either you will hate the one and love the other, or you will be devoted to the one and despise the other. You cannot serve both God and money." Notice that verse 24 specifically talks about how love and devotion can only go to God or to money; the two cannot have equal footing in your life. You can have money but not love it or be devoted to it. If you do, then the love and devotion (worship) that belongs to God is misappropriated in your checking or savings account.

When we return the tithe to God and give him a monetary offering, we prioritize God, declare our devotion to God, and turn our treasure over to Him because our hearts are with Him. Money has a place in our lives; it is essential, and a solution to many things (Ephesians 10:19). But money cannot be our everything. We cannot serve money, we cannot stand in awe of money and give it the respect, honor, and devotion due to God.

Worship Through Song

The worship songs you sing in church or in your car as you drive down the highway are expressions of reverence and adoration of God that have been put to music. When you sing about the holiness of God, His majesty, and His omnipotence, you are humbling yourself at His throne and worshipping God. It is important to note that every positive song about God is not a worship song.

Remember, worship happens in Spirit and in truth. Moreover, worship happens when we sacrifice ourselves and we decrease so God can increase. In worship, God is the focus; we reverence His goodness and character and pour out our love to Him for who He is. Our personal matters, our needs, and our desires go out of focus in worship as we magnify and glorify God. Some songs are about God; they are positive, encourage our hearts, and uplift us, but they are not worship songs.

It is important to make this distinction because God wants to ensure you maintain a posture of worship in your spiritual home, and He does not want you to confuse a positive or feel-good atmosphere with worship. You have to be intentional about humbling yourself and bowing (literally and figuratively) at the throne of God.

Idol Worship

Worship was defined earlier in this chapter, but as a reminder, worship is an expression of reverence (deep respect), adoration(love), and devotion to **something**. Notably, the word **something** tells us that we can worship things other than God. Worshipping anything other than God is idol worship. An idol, by definition, is "an image or representation of a god used as an object of worship (dictionary.com)."

Here is the thing—most people do not acknowledge or admit when they are engaging in idol worship. But the truth is, if you reverence or express deep respect, adoration, or love for a person, place, thing, image, belief, etc., outside of God, you are engaging in idol worship.

You may think—*I deeply love my children.* Is this idol worship? No, a parent's love for their children is natural; children are a reward from God (Psalm 127:3). However, if you place your kids on the throne of your heart, you prioritize them over God, and they receive your complete devotion, you are idolizing your children. Unfortunately, we live in a time where the term idol is used freely and deemed acceptable. Many people openly express they idolize their favorite celebrity, and we have television shows where people compete to be the next idol. However, do not be misled, idol worship is not acceptable. Scripture firmly instructs us, "Do not worship any other god, for the Lord, whose name is Jealous, is a jealous God" (Exodus 34:14, NIV).

God's jealousy is not like human jealousy. His jealousy derives from a deep love for His children and a desperate desire for a relationship with you and me. He is overly protective of you in the most sincere and beautiful way possible, and it pains Him to see you giving your heart, mind, and spirit to something unworthy. God knows that idols are impotent; they do not have the power to heal you, free you, or give you true peace. He knows this because God created all things; therefore, He is fully aware of the limitations of the people, places, and things you worship that are not Him. "For in him all things were created: things in heaven and on earth, visible and invisible, whether thrones or powers or rulers or authorities; all things have been created through him and for him. He is before all things, and in him all things hold together" (Colossians 1:16-17, NIV). God is concerned and displeased when you rely on other people and things to hold you together because He is the only one who can hold you together.

Furthermore, God is the only one worthy of your worship, deep reverence, adoration, and dependency. Revelation 4:11 (NIV) says, "You are worthy, our Lord and God, to receive glory and honor and power, for you created all things, and by your will they were created and have their being." No created thing, including yourself, is worthy of that kind of deference. If you are serving something God created, like the universe, the sun, the moon, the stars, or anything or anyone else, you are being deceived, and your worship is misplaced (Romans 1:25).

Because we are supposed to *be* a house of worship for God, we cannot allow idol worship to occur in our homes. Second Corinthians 6: 16 (NIV) says, "What agreement is there between the temple of God and idols? For we are the temple of the living God. As God has said: 'I will live with them and walk among them, and I will be their God, and they will be my people.'" Is God *your* God? If the answer is yes, there is no room in your spiritual home for any other gods.

I want to be very clear— idol worship is not a light matter. When you identify that idol worship is taking place in your spiritual home, you must move swiftly to tear down those idols and restore true worship to God in your home. When God was speaking to His children, the Israelites, about other gods (idols), He said, "This is what you are to do to them: Break down their altars, smash their sacred stones, cut down their Asherah poles, and burn their idols in the fire. For you are a people holy to the Lord your God. The Lord your God has chosen you out of all the peoples on the face of the earth to be his people, his treasured possession" (Deuteronomy 7:5-6, NIV).

God instructed His children to bring down idols with force! You cannot take a passive posture with anything that is sitting on God's throne, even if you placed it there. Once you identify that you have worshipped created things, your first action is to remove them. What does that look like? Say to God: *God, I acknowledge I have placed _____ above you. I have given it my devotion, affection, and reverence that only belongs to you. Please forgive me for worshipping a created thing instead of you, my Creator. Today, I fall out of agreement with idol worship, and I place you back on the throne. I declare that Jesus is Lord, and He is Lord of my life. And because Jesus is Lord, I will follow His influence and take my instructions from Him. You are God, and God alone. God, let my spiritual home be a house of worship for you and you only.*

Chapter Seven

A HOUSE OF STUDY

*"Your word is a lamp for my feet, a light
on my path." ~ Psalm 119:105* (NIV)

WHEN MY HUSBAND AND I sat at the closing table for our new home, we signed stacks of paperwork and received the keys to our brand-new home. At the closing table, we were also given specific instructions about the utilities for our new home, specifically the lights. Initially, the builder turned on the lights and covered the cost because they were still in the building phase, and lights were needed as the contractors worked at night laying the floors, painting the walls, setting doors, etc. But when the builder turned over the home to us as the homeowners, we were responsible for covering the cost of the lights moving forward. Our home needed light; we could not depend on daylight from the outside to stream on the inside of our home. We needed light inside our home so we could see at all times, day or night.

Similarly, our spiritual homes need light! God is light, and His Word is light. The good news is, unlike our natural home, we do not have to cover the cost of the light. God gives Himself to us freely, but we do have to choose

His light and be intentional about studying His Word so God can light our path. Let's go deeper.

In 1 Peter 2:9 (NIV), we are reminded of who we are: "But you are chosen people, a royal priesthood, a holy nation, God's special possession, that you may declare the praises of him who called you out of darkness into his wonderful light." This verse tells us that God's light is necessary for our spiritual home. We were living in darkness before we accepted Salvation, entered into a relationship with God through Jesus Christ, and invited the Holy Spirit to live in our lives. Now, God has taken possession of our spiritual home and is working on us from the inside so we can walk in His light.

Light dispels darkness. Light and darkness cannot coexist. This is a scientific fact. Once light comes into a room, darkness disappears. We must ensure God's light is always on in our spiritual homes so the darkness we once lived in cannot prevail. I want to pause here. When we hear the word darkness, we often think about witches, satanic forces, villains from the movies, etc. All of these things are examples of darkness. However, I want to stretch your thinking at this moment. In your spiritual home, darkness is anything that is not like God. Darkness is anything that does not line up with God, His Word, and who God has called you to be.

In the book of Ephesians, the Apostle Paul talks about the Gentiles, those outside of God's covenant and not in a relationship with God. And Paul said, "So I tell you this, and insist on it in the Lord, that you must no longer live as the Gentiles do, in the *futility of their thinking*. They are *darkened in their understanding* and separated from the life of God because of the ignorance that is in them due to the hardening of their hearts" (Ephesians 4:17-18, NIV).

The Apostle Paul said the Gentiles were darkened in their understanding and called out their futile, ineffective, empty thinking. He was talking about their thought life. The darkest room in our spiritual home tends to be upstairs, our mind. We need God's light to shine in our minds so we won't be darkened in our thinking or have dark thoughts.

One way that we shine God's light in our home is through studying His Word. God's Word gives us instructions and guidance on how to live a life of faith; it reveals God's character to us, and the Truth of God's Word confronts the lies of the enemy. Too many followers of Jesus Christ are trying to follow Him without studying His Word. We live in a time where the emphasis is placed on Sunday morning experiences at church, propping God up on social media platforms, and having church "swag." Little emphasis is placed on studying God's Word so it can light your path (Psalm 119:105). Moreover, very few people make the connection that the Word is God, and if we don't study the Word, we don't know God. Thus, our Sunday morning church experiences are futile, our social media posts are irrelevant, and our relationships with God are reduced to "swag."

John 1: 1-5 (NIV) is very clear when it reads, "In the beginning was the Word, and the Word was with God, and the Word was God. He was with God in the beginning. Through him all things were made; without him nothing was made that has been made. In him was life, and that life was the **light** of all mankind. The light shines in the darkness and the has not overcome it." Notice how the scripture above personifies the Word; the Word is God. In John 1:14(NIV), John says, "The Word became flesh and made his dwelling among us. We have seen his glory, the glory of the one and only Son, who came from the Father, full of grace and truth." You read the verse, but let's reread it because you have to make the connection, "The Word **became flesh and made his dwelling among us**. We have seen his glory, **the glory of the one and only Son, who came from the Father**, full of grace and truth."

The Word is Jesus! The Word is not just books written by man. The Word is God-breathed, and from cover to cover, the pages of the Bible point you to Jesus. You may be thinking that *Jesus doesn't even arrive on the scene until the New Testament portion of the Bible.* This is not true. First John 1:1 tells us Jesus was with God from the beginning.

We have to dig deeper into scripture to make this connection fully. Jesus said, "I and the Father are one" (John 10:30, NIV). So, the Word is both God and Jesus because they are one. It is important to note that the Word (Jesus) was the Word in the beginning, before there was paper or ink and before there was a written Word. The Holy Bible encapsulates the Word, chronicles the acts of God, captures His character on paper, details the lives of His people, and gives us His divine direction for our lives. However, from the beginning, God, Jesus (the Word), and the Spirit of God (the Holy Spirit) were here.

When you study the Word by reading your Bible, you gain the truth about God *and* Jesus because they are one. Biblical truths teach you about God and illuminate every room in your spiritual home, even the rooms where darkness is comfortable. Bible study cannot be optional for you. If you do not study the Holy Bible, you will not know the Word, Jesus (who is one with God). And if you do not know God, your home will lack the light that you need to glorify God with your being.

What does it mean to study the Bible? It is more than listening to a Sunday morning sermon or listening to the preached word via podcast. The preached word is essential to your spiritual growth and development, but it cannot compensate for you studying the Bible for yourself. When you study something, you develop an intimacy with the topic that can only come from you personally devoting time to learning the topic.

Study, by definition, is to devote time and attention to acquiring knowledge on a subject, especially using books (dictionary.com). We acquire knowledge about the Word (Jesus) through studying the Bible. For many, we don't have a strong appetite for Bible study. Transparently, it can feel like a difficult read; the information does not always make sense, and it can be hard to relate to what we are reading in scripture. That's understandable, but don't let that deter you from Bible study. Ask God to give you an appetite for studying His word. Ask Him to stir up a passion for personal Bible study, to give you an understanding of what you are reading, and to reveal Himself to you as you read His scriptures.

Your enemy, the devil, does not want you to devote time and attention to the Bible. Why? Because he knows it will teach you more about God the Father and Jesus the Son. The devil also knows God's Word is Truth, and the Truth sets you free (John 8:32). Free from what? Free from the bondage of sin and the lies the enemy has told you all your life. The enemy also recognizes the more you know about God, the more light shines in your spiritual home and dispels darkness. The devil operates in darkness, and his kingdom is darkness. The light of the Word penetrates his darkness and usurps the devil's power in your life.

With this understanding, you must be bent, determined, and insistent on studying the Bible. We all have taken classes in the past that we had to pass because our graduation, certification, or licensure depended on them. It is with that same fervor and desperation that we have to study the Word. Our spiritual homes depend on it, our relationship with God cannot thrive without it, and our freedom in Christ is in jeopardy if we do not study the Word.

There are many tools to help you study the Bible more effectively. There are study Bibles that give you historical context before the beginning of every book; they give you details on the people, the place, and the author before you jump into the scriptures ahead. This is helpful because you need background when you truly aim to learn about God through His scriptures. The scriptures take on a new meaning when you know who wrote the book of the Bible you are reading, why they wrote it, the historical events that were happening during that time that influenced the scriptures, etc.

Men wrote the Bible, but it is God-breathed. It is useful for teaching, rebuking, correcting, and training (2 Timothy 3:16). Even though the written Word of God is thousands of years old, we depend on its teaching today because it does not lose relevance; it is a living word. "For the word of God is alive and active" (Hebrews 4:12, NIV). This means the scriptures can speak to us today and light our paths.

I will repeat this at the risk of being redundant: **you cannot glorify God with your being if you do not know God.** Therefore, Bible study cannot be an optional activity in your home. Again, if you do not enjoy Bible study, ask God to ignite your passion for the Bible. If the passion for studying the Word has not come yet, study anyway. The Apostle Paul talks about the discipline needed to truly glorify God with your being. He likens serving God to running a race and says, "Do you not know that in a race, all the runners run, but only one gets the prize? Run in such a way as to get the prize. Everyone who competes in the games goes into strict training. They do it to get a crown that will not last, but we do it to get a crown that will last forever. Therefore, I do not run like someone aimlessly; I do not fight like a boxer beating the air. No, I strike a blow to my body and make it my slave so that after I have preached to others, I myself will not be disqualified for the prize" (1 Corinthians 9:24-27, NIV).

Paul is speaking to the discipline required in our spiritual homes, the practice and training, and the commitment we have to have when it comes to God. You have to practice studying the Bible and commit to this practice daily. First Timothy 1:7(NIV) says, "For the Spirit God gave us does not make us timid, but gives us power, love, and self-discipline." The Spirit of God, who lives inside our homes, will help you. He will give you the discipline, direction, and regimen needed for Bible study, but you have to want it. To be filled, you must hunger and thirst for righteousness (Matthew 5:6).

I will say it again: **you cannot glorify God with your being if you do not know God.** Knowing God is the point! You know God through Jesus (John 14:6). The Bible is how you get to know God through Jesus. The Apostle Paul said it this way, "What is more, I consider everything a loss because of the surpassing worth of knowing Christ Jesus my Lord, for whose sake I lost all things. I consider them garbage, that I may gain Christ" (Philippians 3:8, NIV). Knowing Christ is the point—Not church swag, not having the appearance of godliness on social media while lacking His power, not looking for blessings, not seeking God for a spouse, not gaining followers on your socials, not acquiring wealth. Paul considered all these things a loss because they do not compare with the worth or the value of knowing Christ Jesus.

The Apostle Paul went on to say, "I want to know Christ-yes, to know the power of his resurrection and participation in his sufferings, becoming like him in his death, and so, somehow, attaining to the resurrection from the dead" (Philippians 3:10-11, NIV). Paul is saying, I want to know Christ and the power of his resurrection! Why? Because that same resurrection power can come alive in my life! When you study the Bible, you learn about Jesus and the power of His resurrection. That resurrection power will bring life to your spiritual home!

I can personally testify that there were aspects of my life that were spiritually dead. I've experienced dead emotions (depression), lifeless relationships, unproductive thoughts, and weariness in my spirit. But the Word of God (Jesus) came into those dead places and resurrected them! When I read the written Word of God, the Truth comes into my home, and the power of Jesus transforms my heart and mind. Resurrection and transformation cannot take place in your spiritual home without the knowledge of Christ.

So much has been said about Bible study in this chapter, but I leave you with this: you have been wondering what is missing and why things aren't working. You have put effort into having a relationship with God, you have been more diligent about attending church services, you are choosing different people to hang with because you know that bad company corrupts good character (1 Corinthians 15:33). You are actively laying aside your addictions, giving up your vices, and purposing in your heart to serve God. Still, it's not coming together, it's not working. You are not experiencing the fruit of your labor. Your relationship with God is lacking and you don't feel a closeness with Him and aren't experiencing His presence and power in your life. If you are not studying your Bible regularly, that is what is missing.

Think about it like this: if you are a student who registers for a class, gets your textbooks, has a bookbag, and goes to class, but you never study the material, you will not succeed in that class because you lack knowledge. Maybe you didn't understand the importance of personal Bible study before you read this chapter, but now you do. Your spiritual home will be dark, dank, and empty without the light of God's Word and the power that comes from knowing Jesus Christ.

Chapter Eight

A HOUSE OF PRAYER

"Pray Continually." ~ 1 Thessalonians
5:17 (NIV)

OUR SPIRITUAL HOME SHOULD be a house of prayer just like it is a house of worship and study. Yes, you should physically go to your local church and pray there, but 1 Thessalonians 5:17 makes it very clear that *we* should pray continually.

To give context, the book of 1 Thessalonians is the Apostle Paul's letter to the church in Thessalonica (the modern-day Greek city of Thessaloniki). This city was the capital of the Roman province of Macedonia, and it was a port city, which means it had a strong economy. Though many of the people were Greek, there were diverse cultures. To put it simply, Thessalonica was like today's New York City.

I share all of that so you understand the audience Paul is speaking to when he says, "Pray continually." He is speaking to people who are surrounded by competing priorities like commerce, social activities, and culture. Sound familiar? He is speaking to people who were seeking to follow the teaching of Jesus amid staunch religious teachers who were telling them to pattern their lives after the bylaws of Moses, admonishing them to be performative in their Faith and to look the part of a believer on the inside while ignoring the transformation that needed to take place on the inside in their hearts, mind, and spirit. Sound familiar? Paul also speaks to people who regularly had to contend with false teachings that diluted the gospel of Jesus Christ, in effect telling the Thessalonians that it 'doesn't take all of that.' These false teachers were permitting them to relax their moral standards. Sound familiar?

Paul says, "Pray continually" to those who were purposing in their hearts to follow and look like Jesus amid religious misinformation, chaos, and culture. That same instruction applies to us today.

Prayer is not an option for the person who wants to glorify God with their being. Prayer, put simply, is talking to God. But be very clear: while the act of prayer is simple, the effect of prayer is powerful! When you open your mouth and speak to your Father (God), who is in heaven, earth interacts with heaven. When you pray to God, the Creator of the Universe (Genesis 1:1), the All-Mighty One (Psalm 62:7), and the Great King (Psalm 95:3), you are engaging heaven, and the results are supernatural, indescribable, and beyond comprehension!

You may think *my prayers don't feel that deep or impactful.* My response is that you have yet to experience the power of prayer. James 5:13 tells us the prayers of a righteous person are powerful and effective!

Perhaps you haven't experienced the power of prayer because you have only prayed in one lane; your prayers are strictly petitions to God. Or perhaps you haven't experienced the power of prayer because you have been praying in your name instead of sealing the conversation with the name of Jesus. Let's take some time and dig into prayer to ensure that your spiritual home is a house where powerful and effective prayer is taking place continually at all times.

Jesus Taught His Disciples How to Pray

When Jesus walked this Earth in human form, He walked with His disciples and taught them many things. One lesson He taught them was how to pray. In Matthew 6, Jesus gave His followers specifics about prayer. Whenever you find Jesus going in-depth on a topic, that should alert you that the topic is important. That means you need to learn, take in every part of Jesus' instruction, and willfully and intentionally apply the truth of Jesus' words in your life. Let's unpack the Truth around prayer.

Jesus said, "And when you pray, do not be like the hypocrites, for they love to pray standing in the synagogues and on the street corners to be seen by others. Truly, I tell you, they have received their reward in full. But when you pray, go into your room, close the door and pray to your Father, who is unseen. Then the Father, who sees what is done in secret, will reward you" (Matthew 6:5-6, NIV).

Jesus was cautioning His disciples not to engage in performative prayer, praying to be noticed by others. Prayer is not an exercise to see who is most spiritual. I mentioned earlier that the Thessalonian people lived amongst some religious leaders who encouraged performative faith. More specifically, they lived amongst Pharisees, a group who built their lives on following the written laws outlined by Moses (Exodus 20) and rejected the life of Faith and grace through Jesus Christ.

Pharisees were bent on performing religious duties and having the appearance of righteousness and right living, but they were only spiritual in their behavior, not in their hearts. Jesus was speaking of the Pharisees when he said, "Woe to you, teachers of the law and Pharisees, you hypocrites! You clean the outside of the cup and dish, but inside, they are full of greed and self-indulgence. Blind Pharisee! First, clean the inside of the cup and dish, and then the outside also will be clean" (Matthew 23:25-26), NIV.

Notice that Jesus called the Pharisees, those who were fixed on religious dogma, <u>hypocrites</u>. Now, let's go back to Jesus' teaching on prayer. Jesus said don't pray like the <u>hypocrites</u> do, don't pray simply out of religious duty, don't pray for public appeal and applause. When *you* pray, as a follower of Jesus Christ, pray with the intent to speak to your Father in Heaven. Prayer is how we engage our Father in heaven. That is why Jesus said not to pray standing in the synagogues or on the street corners but instead to pray privately in your room. This is not to say public prayer is not allowed, but public prayer should only be a continuation of the prayers that take place within the privacy of your spiritual home.

Let's go back to Jesus' conversation with His disciples. He went on to say, "And when you pray, do not keep on babbling like the pagans, for they think they will be heard because of their many words. Do not be like them, for your Father knows what you need before you ask" (Matthew 6:7-8, NIV).

There are a couple of takeaways from these two scriptures. First, prayer is not about meeting a specific word count. Do not feel that your prayers need to be a certain length. The key is to speak to God in your authentic voice and that your prayers are specific and targeted, especially when petitioning God for something. I am a mom, and I am sure you can relate if you are a parent. At times, when your children enter the room, you know they want something, and you have a pretty good idea of what they want. You, like me, listen as they talk around the subject of their request, make small talk, and insert humor into the conversation as they ramp up to making their request known.

Jesus said, don't do that. Don't ramble on when you pray to God, especially if you need something from Him, because He, like earthly parents, knows exactly what you need. He is just waiting for you to open your mouth and articulate your ask to Him. It is also important to note that even if you are not petitioning heaven for something, you should communicate directly with God. Heaven takes receipt of your prayers. So, pray with clarity and boldness.

Last year, I joined the Prayer and Care team at my church. I say I joined, but truly, I accepted the call to be a part of this squad of intercessory prayer warriors who are committed to bombarding heaven with prayers for our families, our ministry, the community, and beyond! Before I accepted the call to be on the Prayer and Care team, I prayed, but since joining the team, my prayers have taken a different shape. I understand more fully that my prayers are not just leaving my lips and landing in the cosmos or, worse, on a deaf ear. God hears my prayers and pleas and upholds my cause (2 Chronicles 6:24-35). Moreover, God is *attentive,* and He hears the prayers that I offer to Him (2 Chronicles 6:40).

When you grasp that truth, that God is attentively listening to you when you speak, your prayer life will shift! You will be more inclined to speak to God from your heart, desire to be more precise in your conversation with Him, and be compelled to pray more frequently.

Let's continue to unpack Jesus' instructions surrounding prayer. Jesus continued to speak to the disciples and gave them the model for prayer. He said, "This, then, is how you should pray: 'Our Father in heaven, hallowed be your name, your kingdom come, your will be done, on earth as it is in heaven. Give us today our daily bread. And forgive us our debts, as we also have forgiven our debtors. And lead us not into temptation but deliver us from the evil one" (Matthew 6:9-13, NIV).

This prayer has been coined the "Lord's Prayer." Maybe you learned it in Sunday school, or you and your parents knelt beside your bed at night and prayed it together before you went to sleep. This prayer can be prayed verbatim daily, but even when you do not pray these exact words, these principles should be captured in your everyday prayers.

Jesus begins His prayer by saying, "Our Father in Heaven, hallowed by your name" (Matthew 6:9, NIV). With this phrase, Jesus demonstrates that we should show reverence to God when we pray. It is not about lofty language or conjuring up the biggest words you know. Reverence for God is a matter of spiritual posture. Yes, you should boldly approach God's throne when you pray (Hebrews 4:16). You do not have to pray from a place of timidity or shame. However, when you open your mouth to pray to your Father in heaven, there is deep respect and acknowledgment that you should have for God, understanding you have the opportunity to commune with the Creator of the universe, the God who knew you before *you* knew you (Jeremiah 1:5). You are conversing with the One who set the world in motion; The God who said let there be light, and there was light. This God is giving you the floor to speak with Him (Genesis 1:1-3). God, who parted the Red Sea so His children could escape from their oppressors on dry land, is giving you space to engage with Him (Exodus 14:21).

When you breathe in the fact that God is bigger, more powerful, more supreme, more righteous, more holy, more.... than anything or anyone you know, you exhale reverence. When you start your prayers with reverence for God and who He is, your conversation with God is altered in the most beautiful way. It humbles you, and it elevates Him. When you approach your prayers with reverence and humility, that's when healing takes place for you and for those you pray for; that's when God's power lifts your prayer life.

Jesus continued His instruction on prayer and said, "Your kingdom come, your will be done, on earth as it is in heaven" (Matthew 6:10, NIV). This is key for every prayer that we pray. We have to shape our prayers around God's will. Too often, we approach God as if He were a genie, and our prayers are just our way of 'rubbing the lamp' to get God to carry out our will and our wishes. God hears us when we pray and upholds our cause, but He does that when our cause, interests, and principles align with His.

God is sovereign; He is absolute, and His character is unwavering (Hebrews 13:8). God will not deviate from His character to honor your prayer. For example, God is Love (1 John 4:8), so He will not step outside of His Love to punish someone the way you want someone to be punished, even if you pray for Him to do so. Instead, He will have mercy on whom He wants to have mercy on (Romans 9:18), and He will repay wrong in the manner He deems appropriate (Hebrews 10:30).

I recognize that is not what you want to hear, but you will receive God's truth and honesty in this book. Unfortunately, God's children have been conned into believing we can direct God's hand, and we have weaponized prayer to provoke God to do as we see fit in our lives. However, God will only move in accordance with His will.

Moreover, God's thoughts are above our thoughts, and His ways above our ways (Isaiah 55:9), so he cannot pander to every instruction you give Him in prayer because He sees the bigger picture. And sometimes you want to hear "Yes" to your prayer when the divine answer is "No" or "Not right now." You have to be okay with that because God is all-knowing. He is a good Father, and he would not withhold a good thing from you (Psalm 84:11). He will, however, shield you from dangers seen and unseen (Psalm 91:7), but you have to trust Him.

So, you may ask, what is the point of praying at all if God will ultimately do what He wills? Prayer is how we communicate with God; every relationship needs communication. Moreover, when we pray prayers aligning with God's Word and His will, God moves! We cannot expect God to move on matters we do not engage Him in. Think about it this way: When my husband and I were ready to buy a home, we knew the time was right, the homesites were available, and we had the necessary funds, but we had to walk into the sales office, speak with the salesperson, and begin the purchase transaction.

Everything was in order for us to buy a home, but there had to be activation on our part.

Prayer activates heaven, and it sets in motion God's prepared plans. You may be thinking, *I don't know the will of God. How can I pray prayers that line up with His will?* You will find the will of God in the written Word of God. The last chapter focused on the importance of Bible study. When you study God's Word and learn more about Jesus Christ, you better understand His thoughts, intentions for you and your family, His Promises, and His plans, which will help shape your prayer life.

When you study the Bible and get to know Christ, you also take on His heart and posture. God's Holy Spirit, living on the inside of you, will give you the desires of your heart (Psalm 37:4). God will literally give you what to desire, and when that happens, you know your prayers will align with God's will and Heaven's agenda.

Jesus continued His teaching on prayer and said, "Give us today our daily bread" (Matthew 6:11. NIV). In saying this, Jesus tells His disciples to make sure you pray in the present. That is not to say you can't pray for future events or outcomes; however, He wanted them to be intentional about praying for what they need at that moment because tomorrow has enough trouble of its own (Matthew 6:34). We all could benefit from praying in the present for the present.

Also, Jesus taught them to depend on God daily. You ask God for *today's* bread. Jesus told His disciples in John 6: 35 (NIV), "I am the bread of life. Whoever comes to me will never go hungry, and whoever believes in me will never be thirsty."

Jesus told them that He is the bread of life, and when you pray, seek Him and seek Him daily. And know that when you seek Jesus first every day, all of the other things that you want and need will be added to you (Matthew

6:33). You can pray for things, but when you daily seek the bread of life, Jesus, the things come as complimentary add-ons.

Jesus continued by telling the disciples that their prayers should include asking God for forgiveness, "And forgive us our debts, as we forgive our debtors" (Matthew 6:12, NIV). Earlier in this book, we talked about how Jesus' death on the cross and His resurrection freed us from the grip of sin and the penalty of death. However, we also said that we all will sin (Romans 3:23). With that clarity, we should ask God to forgive us for our sins regularly. A good place to start is, *"Lord, I am not perfect. Please forgive me for all of my sins."* This is an excellent place to start, but calling out your specific sins is a better place to land.

In Hebrews 12:1 (NIV), we are instructed to "lay aside every weight, and the sin which so easily ensnares us." You cannot lay aside sins you do not identify and call out. Think about it like this: we all have received an apology from someone that sounds something like, "I'm sorry." You may follow up that type of apology with the question, "Sorry for what?" From there, the individual may say, "I'm sorry that you were upset by what I did." We all hate those apologies; they really lay the responsibility for the hurt on the recipient of the pain versus the perpetrator. Also, the apology is vague and doesn't speak to the specific hurtful behavior.

A more vulnerable, sincere, and ideal apology sounds like, "I apologize for raising my voice when I spoke to you. I understand that it hurt your feelings, AND I will do my best never to raise my voice with you again." Notice that the ideal apology specifies the person's hurtful action, and the person commits to avoiding that behavior in the future. Why am I giving this example about apologies? Too often, we ask God for blanket forgiveness. We don't expose our sin; subsequently, we don't lay aside our sin, which continues to ensnare us.

When you get specific with God about your sin, you bring it out of darkness and into God's light. It's not about being self-deprecating or wallowing in condemnation; it is about being transparent with God and asking Him to forgive you for being judgmental towards your husband, abrasive with your kids, disrespectful to your leader at work, rude to the coffee shop barista, etc. And when you ask God for forgiveness, you repent, express remorse for your behavior, and commit to laying aside those behaviors.

It is important to note that when Jesus instructed the disciples to ask for forgiveness in prayer, He also said to be sure to forgive others, "And forgive us our debts, **as we forgive our debtors** "(Matthew 6:12, NIV). The necessity to forgive others is something that cannot be overlooked. We discussed forgiveness earlier in the book, but let's go deeper into this topic. First, we forgive others because God so graciously forgives us. Ephesians 4:32 (NIV) says it this way, "Be kind and compassionate to one another, forgiving each other, just as in Christ God forgave you."

We are further admonished in Colossians 1:13 (NIV): "For he has rescued us from the dominion of darkness and brought us into the kingdom of the Son he loves, in whom we have redemption, the forgiveness of sins." We are unworthy recipients of God's grace and His forgiveness. With that understanding, we freely forgive others, whether or not we feel they are worthy of our forgiveness. We do not withhold forgiveness because forgiveness was not withheld from us.

You may be reading this part of this book, and you feel something telling you: *I am not going to forgive. I am reading this, and I get it, but I am not going to forgive. They do not deserve my forgiveness.* Let me alert you that you have an intruder in your home, and their name is Pride. I do not know you, and I do not know the situation or the pain they caused you, but God does. He is all-knowing, and even with complete information and details on your situation, God is telling you to forgive.

Pride stands in opposition to forgiveness. Pride convinces you that you are worthy of forgiveness daily but that the person who wronged you is not worthy of your forgiveness. You can always tell when pride is present because it builds you up (you are always the hero) and tears others down (they are always the villain). It is not without reason that scripture says, "Pride goes before destruction, a haughty spirit before a fall" (Proverbs 16:18, NIV).

Pride is judgmental; it makes you believe that hurting others is a light offense and that people should understand your heart and intentions. Meanwhile, when others hurt you, there is no room for grace because their offense is great, and clearly, they intended to be hurtful. Pride is also in conflict with God's love. First Corinthians 13:5 (NIV) tells us about love: "It does not dishonor others, it is not self-seeking, it is not easily angered, it keeps no record of wrongs."

I do not call out pride to point the finger at you, but I do want to point the finger at it. We have to identify intruders when they show up in our spiritual home so we can evict them. I know you are hurt and that forgiveness doesn't feel like the formula to address your hurt, but you have to forgive. Forgiving others is also essential to maintain peace in your spiritual home. I am sure you have heard it said before that forgiveness is not for the other person but for you. That statement could not be more accurate. As we discussed earlier, when we choose to withhold forgiveness, we give bitterness space in our spiritual homes. You may be thinking what I once thought, *"I'm not bitter. I just refuse to let someone wrong me or walk over me and think it's okay."*

To be clear, forgiveness is not about allowing someone to walk over you; it is about not allowing a person or a situation to bind you. When you choose to forgive someone, it is not about rewriting the narrative or convincing yourself the offense did not hurt you. It is also not about justifying the wrong someone committed against you. Forgiveness does, however, release you from carrying the weight of the hurt they caused, and you insist on peace in your spiritual home.

It is not without reason that Hebrews 12: 14-15 (NIV) tells us to "Make every effort to live in peace with everyone and to be holy; without holiness, no one will see the Lord. See to it that no one falls short of the grace of God and that no bitter root grows up to cause trouble and defile many."

There is so much truth and clarity in those two verses alone! When peace is lacking in our spiritual home, we lack the ability to live holy, set-apart lives that glorify God. Moreover, when we don't extend forgiveness and grace to others, we create a gap in our relationship with God because we are trying to engage with a God who, by nature, is forgiving, yet we are choosing to be unforgiving.

Think about it like this: have you ever tried to be in a relationship with someone whose character was misaligned with yours? The disparity in your characters created a disconnect between the two of you and usually resulted in conflict. When we forgive, we take on God's character and His nature, ensuring that we don't fall short in our relationship with Him and create a disconnect between us.

When we don't forgive others, we also position ourselves to miss God's grace and forgiveness for our sins. I am skipping ahead in our scripture text, but Matthew 6:14 (NIV) tells us, "For if you forgive other people when they sin against you, your Heavenly Father will also forgive you. But if you do not forgive others their sins, your Father will not forgive you." This scripture by itself should compel you to forgive others. Whatever someone did to upset or hurt you is unfortunate enough, but to allow that person, those people, that moment, and that situation to cause you to miss out on the forgiveness you need from God is unbearable. It compounds the situation.

You and I should be bent on protecting our relationship with our Father. And since we know that God will not forgive us our sins when we don't forgive others, we should insist on forgiving if for no other reason than we do not want to fall out with our Father behind someone, their foolishness, or their inability to treat us the way we wanted or needed to be treated.

As we discussed earlier in the book, when we forgive, we protect our home from being defiled by the root of bitterness. The Greek word for bitterness is pikría, and it means bitter gall. More plainly, it is likening bitterness to the contents of the gallbladder, bile, in your innermost parts. This kind of bitterness is also likened to extreme wickedness and hatred. Pikría, bitter gall, produces a bitter root in your innermost being, producing bitter fruit.

That is why **forgiveness is a must in your spiritual life.** You cannot allow any space for bitterness to take root in your home, to curdle your insides, and produce hate and bitter fruit. Bitter gall defiles your spiritual home and stains your relationship with God. This is why the Scripture warns us, "Do not take revenge, my dear friends, but leave room for God's wrath, for it is written, "It is mine to avenge; I will repay says the Lord" (Romans 12:19, NIV). It is not about giving your offenders a pass but protecting your spiritual home from bitter gall.

You may be thinking, *I hear this, I get this, but I don't even know where to begin when it comes to forgiving others.* You start with prayer, yet another reason why prayer is so important. When you talk to God, you release all of your pain to Him. You even ask Him to show you where you buried the trauma, bypassed healing, or became numb to the hurt. You do this in prayer, with God in the room, because this is difficult stuff. In prayer, you cast your cares on God, and when I say cast your cares on God, I mean put all of your weight on Him. Have you ever sat on someone's lap or a chair and tried to shift your weight in such a way that your entire body weight was not felt?

This is not that. When you take your pain to God, you give Him the full extent of you. Once you do that, you choose to forgive others in prayer. Literally, you say, *"God, I choose to forgive_____."* I want to warn you that when you choose to forgive, you may not feel an immediate difference or walk away from that prayer wanting to hug your offender. However, you have given God access to that room in your home. The room that was occupied by the pain of your past, or the resentment about how they treated you, or the guilt for your own wrongdoing is now occupied by God. And when God occupies a place, He stretches out in that space and changes things as only He can.

Forgiving others and yourself is a choice; you may have to stand by your decision to forgive more than once. We would like to believe that forgiveness is a one-and-done exercise, but we have to walk out forgiveness daily. Going back to pikría, bitter gall. If a person, place, or thing so injured you, so impacted you, so hurt you that it got into your bile, your innermost parts, it may take some time for your system to be cleansed. But God is the cleanser. With the Holy Spirit residing in your home (He is Truth), with worship taking place in your spiritual home (worshipping Him in spirit and in Truth), and when you are studying God's word in your home (God's Word is Truth), you will get an overdose of the Truth which will cleanse the bitter gall and set you free. "They shall know the truth and the truth will set you free" (John 8:32, NIV).

Jesus concluded His instruction on prayer with, "And lead us not into temptation, but deliver us from the evil one" (Matthew 6:13, NIV). Jesus told His disciples that when you pray, you should proactively pray against the schemes of your enemy, the evil one, the devil. God does not tempt us (James 1:13), but as discussed earlier in the book, we are tempted by our own fleshly desires and the enemy. Within the course of the day, we are all tempted to say or do something that does not glorify God; we are all tempted to offer a natural response to situations that call for restraint and spiritual wisdom. The temptation to act outside of God's character is ongoing.

Jesus instructs us to pray proactively about temptation. What does that sound like? Well, my prayer sounds like this, *"God, please be with me today. Be in every room I walk into, in every conversation I have, and in every action I do. I need you. When people see me, let them see you. Let me be light in dark places today and look like you. Please let your Holy Spirit lead and guide me today so I don't do or say anything that is not like you. Jesus is my Lord; He will influence my decisions today; I will take my direction from Him and no one else."* When I pray this prayer, I am praying for God to be in the driver's seat so temptation and the evil one (the devil) cannot have that seat.

Transparently, I just started praying that specific prayer at the end of last year, and I try to make it a point to pray that prayer every morning. We are not perfect; God does not expect perfection. However, proactively praying against the enemy's temptation tactics positions you to experience victory through Jesus every day.

Different Types of Prayers

Jesus gave the model of prayer; we just discussed that. However, there are different types of prayers, and you pray depending on the situation. For example, there are prayers of thanksgiving. Colossians 4:2 (NIV) says, "Devote yourselves to prayer, being watchful and thankful." You have something to thank God for every day; you should say a "Thank you" prayer every day throughout the day.

The scripture tells us if someone is sick, we should pray: "Is anyone among you sick? Let them call on the elders of the church to pray over them and anoint them with oil in the name of the Lord. And the prayer offered in faith will make the sick person well" (James 5:14-15). We can call on the elders of the church to pray when we are sick, but *we* can also pray prayers of healing over our own bodies. Matthew 21:22 (NIV) says, "If you believe, you will receive whatever you ask for in prayer." That includes healing from sickness and disease.

As soon as you read that last sentence you possibly thought, *people pray for healing for themselves and other people every day, and people still die.* This is a factual statement, but remember Jesus' teachings on prayer that we discussed earlier. We always pray for God's will to be done in our lives and the lives of others. Yes, we still fervently pray for healing. Jesus was pierced for our transgressions and crushed for our iniquities; he brought us peace, and by his wounds, we are healed (Isaiah 53:5). Healing lines up with God's will. He is a healer (Psalm 103:2-3); however, how and when He chooses to heal is up to Him.

Another type of prayer is a prayer of intercession. These prayers are not for you or about you; they are for others. You are engaging heaven on behalf of someone else. The prayers that take place in your spiritual home should not solely focus on you. Take time at the beginning of your day and throughout your day to pray for your immediate family and extended loved ones. Pray for your church family, your pastors, people in your community, co-workers, and those in government who make decisions that impact you. Pray for the person on the street because you see their situation even if you don't know their name.

Prayers of intercession are game-changing! When you pray for others, you become a mouthpiece for people who don't know God or don't have the know-how or language to approach His throne in prayer. God's Holy Spirit, who lives inside of you, regularly intercedes on your behalf when you don't know the words to pray about something or are unaware of an area in your spiritual home that needs prayer and covering. The Holy Spirit steps in and prays to God for you (Romans 8:26-27). We, in turn, should intercede for others.

When we pray, we should also pray prayers of protection for our spiritual home. Ephesians 6:10-11 lays out the spiritual armor of God. As you know, we are in a spiritual battle every day. Every day, we rely on God's Holy Spirit living inside us; we seek God's truth so the light of His truth will dispel darkness, and we identify intruders who try to occupy space in our spiritual home. With that in mind, we need to put on the spiritual armor of God in prayer so our spiritual homes can be protected and secure.

This spiritual armor is not physical but spiritual because our struggle is not physical but spiritual. "For our struggle is not against flesh and blood, but against the rulers, against the authorities, against the powers of this dark world and against the spiritual forces of evil in the heavenly realms" (Ephesians 6:12, NIV). Understanding this, **every day,** you need to put on the whole armor of God in prayer.

Every piece of armor has a very specific purpose, and it guards a particular part of your spiritual home.

The Belt Of Truth

"Stand firm then, with the belt of truth buckled around your waist..." (Ephesians 6:14, NIV). Similar to how a belt fastens you in and holds your garments together, the Truth of God does the same thing—it anchors us. The Truth is God is the only true and living God (Jeremiah 10:10). The Truth is Jesus is Lord (Romans 10:9, Philippians 2:9). The Truth is that God loves us, and He sent Jesus to die for our sins (John 3:16). The Truth is the blood of Jesus redeemed us, and God forgives us (Ephesians 1:7).

When you fasten the belt of Truth around your waist every day, you align with the Truth about God and the Truth about who He says you are. You are fearfully and wonderfully made (Psalm 139:14). You are loved by God (John 3:16). You are God's chosen and treasured possession (1 Peter 2:9, 2 Corinthians 4:7). The belt of Truth helps you hold these things together each day, so you don't align with the lies of the devil, culture, or even the lies you tell yourself. This is why John 17:17 (NIV) says, "We are sanctified, set apart by God's truth." The Truth sanctifies us; it sets us apart from the deception we are confronted with daily, deception about who God truly is, how God sees us, and who He has called us to be.

Breastplate Of Righteousness

The breastplate of righteousness (Ephesians 6:14) protects our core and vital organs, especially our heart. Remember, this is spiritual armor, so when I say the breastplate of righteousness protects your heart, I am not talking about your physical heart that pumps blood through your body but the intangible organ positioned within your soul's core. I am talking about the heart that has secrets that only God knows (Psalms 44:21). The heart that is deceitful above all things (Jeremiah 17:9). The heart that can be calloused (Isaiah 6:10) but can also be happy (Proverbs 15:13).

The heart that is seated in your soul needs daily protection because the heart can be fickle, and it is not righteous. Therefore, we cover it with the breastplate of righteousness. Every day, we put on the righteousness of Christ to protect this vulnerable place in our spiritual home. Scripture tells us, "God made him [Jesus] who had no sin to be in for us, so that in him we might become the righteousness of God" (2 Corinthians 5:21).

Our heart cannot produce the righteousness that is needed to have an intimate relationship with God; our righteousness is filthy rags (Isaiah 64:6). So, we put on the breastplate of righteousness so it can extend righteousness where we are lacking. God said, "The fruit of that righteousness will be peace; its effect will be quietness and confidence forever. My people will live in peaceful dwelling places, in secure homes, and undisturbed places of rest" (Isaiah 31:18, NIV).

If you do not put on the breastplate of righteousness, you will not experience peace and rest because you will open to the enemy's daily accusations that "you are not good enough, you keep messing up, you are unworthy, and God is mad at you." I know I can't be the only person who hears those thoughts. Let me tell you, they come from the devil. One of the devil's primary jobs is to accuse, condemn, and make you feel worthless. You must daily put on the righteousness of Christ, so your heart is not exposed and susceptible to the enemy's lies and so you can experience God's peace.

I am not sure if you have noticed or not, but there has been an uptick in people dying of heart attacks. While I recognize these deaths have a physical and medical connection to them, I can't help but wonder if there is a spiritual connection. If these physical deaths that we are seeing are evidence of deeper spiritual attacks of the heart. This further points to the need for the breastplate of righteousness.

Gospel Of Peace

"And with your feet fitted with the readiness that comes from the gospel of peace" (Ephesians 6:15, NIV). Notice the word readiness. Readiness means the state of being fully prepared for something. This piece of armor talks about wearing the Gospel of Peace, like shoes, and walking in peace daily. This piece of armor is extremely critical to the believer who wants to glorify God with their body and their entire being. Why? Because God is a God of peace (1 Corinthians 14:33).

With that in mind, we must be fully prepared to **choose** peace every day. We are admonished to take it a step further and to "seek peace and **pursue it**" (Psalms 34:14, NIV). We are instructed in Hebrews to "Make every effort to live in peace with everyone" (Hebrews 12:14). Matthew 5:9 (NIV) tells us, "Blessed are the peacemakers, for they will be called the children of God."

So, you can see, fitting our feet with peace and walking in peace daily is not a suggestion; it is a command for the children of God, for you and me.

Now, I want to be clear: this peace that we walk in daily is not that faux peace, #unbothered. This peace is the Gospel of Peace. It is a peace that comes directly from God. It is an uncommon peace that surpasses understanding (Philippians 4:7). It surpasses understanding because it comes from God. Isaiah 26:12 (NIV)says it this way, "Lord, you establish peace for us; all that we have accomplished you have done for us." We live in a time when people feed on chaos, confusion, and conflict. We need God's peace now more than ever.

Shield Of Faith

"In addition to all this take up the shield of faith, with which you can extinguish all the flaming arrows of the evil one" (Ephesian 6:16, NIV). Our enemy, the devil, knows without faith, it is impossible to please God (Hebrews 11:6). The enemy also knows we have been saved by grace through faith (Ephesians 2:8). Understanding that, the devil is constantly attacking your faith. He is not attacking your faith for a new car, a spouse, or a promotion.

He specifically aims his flaming arrows at your faith in God. All of the pieces of armor are interconnected, but the shield of faith and the belt of truth are especially connected. Your faith in the Truth about God is what is under attack daily. The enemy uses life's circumstances to weaken your trust in God and to deteriorate your faith. He sets up idols in your life so you will place your faith in created things instead of God.

We are justified through faith (Romans 8:1). Scripture tells us, "In him [Jesus] and through faith in him we may approach God with freedom and confidence" (Ephesians 3:12, NIV). Without faith, we cannot have a confident, secure, and mature relationship with God. This is why we pray and put on the shield of faith daily so we can stand firm in our relationship with God through Jesus.

Helmet of Salvation/Sword of the Spirit

"Take the helmet of salvation and the sword of the Spirit, which is the word of God" (Ephesians 6:17, NIV). God was intentional when he paired these final pieces of armor together. The helmet of Salvation covers our heads. We know that we find Salvation in Jesus Christ. Jesus Christ is the head of the church, his body, of which He is the Savior" (Ephesians 5:23, NIV). Christ is our covering, and we don't ever want to approach our day or our life uncovered.

The Sword of the Spirit is the Word of God. In Chapter Six, we talked about the importance of Bible Study. This piece of armor, the Sword of the Spirit, punctuates why we need to study God's written word. In spiritual warfare, the Sword of the Spirit is a defensive *and* offensive weapon. When we hear lies from the enemy or ourselves that tells us God is not real, we respond with the Word of God, "But the Lord is the true God; he is the living God, the eternal King" (Jeremiah 10:10, NIV). When a thought tells you that life is not worth living, you respond with the word, "Yes, my soul, rest in God; my hope comes from him" (Psalms 62:5, NIV). This is defense, countering the opposition that comes your way on a daily basis.

The Sword of the Spirit also works offensively and proactively. You can set the tone for your day at the start of your morning by saying, "I will rejoice in the Lord, I will be joyful in God my Savior" (Habakkuk 3:18, NIV), or you might declare that you will not be anxious for anything but will approach every situation with prayer, petition, and thanksgiving (Philippians 4:6). You proactively speak life into your day by reminding the enemy [and yourself] that you are more than a conqueror through Him who loves you (Romans 8:37) and that God always gives us victory through Jesus Christ (1 Corinthians 15:57). You can wield the Word in the face of addiction and bad habits by saying, "I have the right to do anything, but not everything is beneficial. I have the right to do anything, but I will not be mastered by anything" (1 Corinthians 6: 12, NIV).

The helmet of Salvation and the Sword of the spirit are vital pieces, like every piece of armor, that must be applied daily. When you pray for spiritual protection and put on the whole armor of God each day, say this prayer out loud. Some prayers can be inside your head, but this prayer should be said from your lips so it resounds in your spiritual home. This is my daily prayer. I do not pray in the sequence that is noted in the scripture; I put on the armor from head to toe. I pray out loud, *"God, I consciously put on the entire armor of God. I put on the helmet of Salvation, the breastplate of righteousness, the belt of truth is buckled around my waist, my feet are fitted with the readiness that comes from the Gospel of Peace, and I take up the shield of faith and the Sword of the Spirit."*

Do not leave your spiritual home unsecured! Do not leave your home open and vulnerable to daily attacks and intrusion. Attacks will come, and intruders will try to access your home. Still, it will not prosper when you have God's protection plan: "No weapon formed against you will prevail, and you will refute every tongue that accuses you" (Isaiah 54:17, NIV). Your mission to glorify God every day with every part of your being will be thwarted if you do not put on the armor of God and cover your home.

Chapter Nine

A HOUSE OF PEACE

You will keep him in perfect peace, Whose
mind is stayed on You, Because he trusts in
You. ~Isaiah 26:3 (NKJV)

WHEN YOU ARE INTENTIONAL and consistent in your worship of God, Bible study, and prayer, you will experience a house of peace. It is cause and effect. When you reverence God every day, seek Him through His Word, and speak to Him daily, you put your energy, attention, and mind on God as a matter of lifestyle and not an event; this lifestyle produces God's peace in your life. Too many of us are trying to experience a peace that only comes from God while our minds are far from Him; we are fixed and focused on the daily news, social media platforms, our favorite drama series on television, sports, entertainment, etc.

We want the outcome of peace, but we don't engage in behaviors that catalyze peace. I will say it more plainly: it is like wanting a paycheck without working or wanting muscles without lifting. The two things go hand in hand. Your mind has to stay on God to experience the peace that comes from God. I am not talking about faux peace or the appearance of peace, where you take a selfie of yourself at the pool and post it on your socials with the caption #Chillin. Nor am I talking about the kind of peace that is associated with #WineDownWednesday or a day at the spa. The peace that comes from God is the result of having Him in your life because God is peace (1 Corinthians 14:33). That is *true* peace.

When you are committed to a life of worship, Bible study, and prayer, the Lord of peace himself gives you peace at all times in every way (2 Thessalonians 3:16). The peace that God gives is not contingent upon vacation stays, beautiful sunsets, tranquil conditions, or good times. God's peace is pervasive in pain, present in trials, and potent in difficult times. His peace overrides your emotions; it stabilizes you when your life is falling apart at the seams. God's peace is so unreal that it goes beyond your understanding (Philippians 4:7).

Do you want God's peace? The natural response to that question is, *Yes! Of course!* My next question is, are you willing to adopt the lifestyle it takes to experience God's peace in your life? Please pause and answer that question honestly. For most of us, God's peace comes in waves; it comes and goes and is inconsistent, but that is because *we* are inconsistent. We have moments where we turn down the noise of life, and God gets our full attention. Those are the times when our life is humming, we have a confident stride, we feel clear in our decision-making, and peace prevails no matter what or whom we encounter in our day. In stark contrast, on most days, God gets no attention, or our divided attention, at best. Consequently, our lives feel chaotic, fear overwhelms us, our thoughts are jumbled, and our daily experiences with people and life's demands get the best of us.

Life will be life whether you focus on God or not. Bills will be due, you will have more things to do than you have time, and people will say hurtful things; however, God's peace will enable you to experience an exponentially better life because God's peace gives you His perspective on life's experiences, and it comforts you. You find solace in knowing that trouble won't lead to your undoing because you serve a God who is bigger than your trouble. Jesus forewarned His disciples about the troubles they would experience, but he left them with hope when he said, "I have told you these things so that in me you may have peace. In this world you will have trouble. But take heart! I have overcome the world" (John 16:33, NIV). We have that same hope and comfort today. However, we cannot continue to embrace confusion, willfully engage in anxiety-inducing activities, and expect God's peace.

We have to choose not to engage in activities or conversations or be in settings counterproductive to peace. Before you submit your resignation from your job or rescind the annual Thanksgiving invite for family to visit your home, understand what God is saying. He is talking about you and the Holy Spirit taking a critical look at your daily choices, identifying the people, places, or things that disrupt your peace, and choosing not to engage in those things.

For example, I pray, read my Bible, and then exercise in the mornings. I have an elliptical machine at home, and most days, I will work out on my elliptical and watch television. The television is helpful because it distracts me from the burn in my legs and the tiredness that I feel with each stride. I watch sports commentators or some home improvement shows while I work out, but there was a period when I watched a major news network. This news network typically starts at the top of the morning with updates on wars going on overseas, the latest political conflict, missing persons, etc. I was watching it as I worked out, and I did not feel especially depressed or down after watching it, but the Holy Spirit told me you are disrupting the peace that you just accepted during your time in prayer and study of God's Word. I didn't realize it, but the tone of joy, victory, and peace that I established during my time with God was eroded by the chaos I was listening to on the news network.

I am not saying you can never watch the news; the news can be very informative sometimes. However, God's Spirit told me to choose something different to listen to as I started my day. Don't watch something that is going to introduce pain, grief, confusion, and turmoil into the beautiful day God gifted to you. Another example, I was going through my email, and I received a notification about a new show on one of my favorite streaming channels. The show is about true crimes that happened on college campuses across the nation. So, you know I enjoy true crime documentaries. I believe it may be in part because my father was murdered when I was a teenager; his murder went unsolved, and so detective work and solving crimes intrigues me. However, I heard the Holy Spirit say don't watch that show, and when I think about that guidance from His Spirit, it makes perfect sense. I am a mom with one child in college now and another child who will be in college in two years. Sending children to college is hard enough; you have to adjust to them leaving your nest. I don't need a true crime series about on-campus crimes creating anxiety or giving me any additional things to consider.

I share these examples because often, when we think about protecting God's peace in our lives and avoiding things that jeopardize our peace, we leap to big things like leaving our employer or severing a relationship. But we will retain more peace just by changing a television channel, deleting an app on our phone, or avoiding conversations that we know work us up rather than settle us down.

What I love about God's peace is He promises it to us. He says it is ours to have; we just have to keep our minds on Him. When God is the focus in your spiritual home, He guides your mind and *tells you* what things to give your energy to and where to place your focus. Philippians 4:8 (NIV) instructs us, "Finally, brothers and sisters, whatever is true, whatever is noble, whatever is right, whatever is pure, whatever is lovely, whatever is admirable-if anything is excellent or praiseworthy-think about such things."

Not only do you have God's Holy Spirit living on the inside of you, leading and guiding your thoughts and decision-making, but God laid out for you *exactly* where you need to position your thought life. Please familiarize yourself with this list and check your thoughts against it. When you are stuck in a cycle of thoughts, ask yourself if what you are thinking about is true, pure, or lovely. If the answer is no, the idea or the situation you are considering is likely counterproductive to God's promised peace.

You may be thinking, *Life doesn't work like that. We can't spend every day focusing on rainbows and sunshine; life is hard, some days are not lovely, and there is sadness.* You are absolutely right! God is not telling you to only think on the good things and ignore the tough ones. He is, however, telling you to think on the good things, maintain your peace, and give the tough stuff to Him; let Him think on that. This is where peace and thinking on excellent and praiseworthy things meet. First Peter 5:7 (NIV) says, "Cast *all* your anxiety on him because he cares for you." God is not blind or tone-deaf; He knows that life experiences are difficult and sometimes devastating. He is not ignorant of what pain and weakness feel like (Hebrews 4:15). With full knowledge of how hard life can be, God tells us to cast our cares on Him because He wants to sustain us (Psalms 55:2). He wants us to focus on whatever is true, noble, right, pure, lovely, admirable, excellent, and praiseworthy so He can shoulder the hard stuff, the things that produce anxiety in our life and eat away at our peace.

If you are a parent, you know God's position full well. Good parents want to carry the burdens of life and allow their kids to be kids. I never want my kids to be concerned about how the mortgage will be paid or place the responsibility of the car payments on them. Why? Because they are kids, their shoulders aren't broad enough to carry the weight of adult responsibilities, and I want them to relax, have peace, and enjoy being kids. God feels the same way about us as His children. It's not about being negligent in your responsibilities or psyching yourself out by pretending that everything is always good. It is about letting your Heavenly Father be your Father. When you feel defeated on your job, when you feel devastated by your spouse, when your mind is racing with anxious thoughts, take them to your Father in prayer and leave them there. Leave it at His feet, trust Him with your trouble, and choose to focus on what is working in your life. Choose to focus on the fact that you were blessed with another day. Choose to focus on the fact that you have family, even if the family relationships are strained. Choose to focus on and be grateful for your job, even if it's not your dream job. When you do this, you will promote peace in your spiritual home.

Peace must be a priority. If you read this entire chapter and are still convinced that God's peace feels unattainable or it just doesn't feel realistic, let me alert you: you have an intruder in your home. The intruder may just be poor thinking or learned behaviors. You have lived in a loop of intermittent peace, ups and downs, and God's peace doesn't feel tangible. In that case, your flesh is intruding on the peace God promised. Or the intruder may be the devil himself. He always wants to speak more loudly than the Truth of God, and his job is to steal, kill, and destroy (John 10:10).

One of the things the enemy loves to pilfer is God's peace. He recognizes that you cannot be a productive or potent follower of Christ without God's peace. He also knows that you cannot glorify God with your entire being when you lack God's peace. People in your life see God most from the peace that *you* demonstrate in the face of adversity. Peace is God's calling card, and it attracts people to Him when they see it on display in your spiritual home. This is why you must insist on peace, not only for your personal gain but ultimately for God's gain and glory.

Chapter Ten

LIFE THROUGH THE SPIRIT

"Don't be deceived: God is not mocked. For whatever a person sows he will also reap, because the one who sows to his flesh will reap destruction from the flesh, but the one who sows to the Spirit will reap eternal life from the Spirit. Let us not get tired of doing good, for we will reap at the proper time if we do not give up. ~ Galatians 6:7-10 (CSB)

OUR FAMILY HAS LIVED in our new home for a few years now. What a blessing! For the first year or so, we would wake up in the morning and feel like we needed to pinch ourselves because it felt like a dream. We would get goosebumps every time we walked into our beautiful open-concept kitchen. The new paint smell gave us all the "new-home feelings." Every time we pulled into our driveway, our hearts overflowed with gratitude because this was our very own home! It wasn't one of the many model homes that we toured; it belonged to us!

Now that we are three years in, we have to be more intentional about taking a step back, taking in the features of our home, and expressing gratitude to God. We still live in our home, love its features, and are still grateful to be homeowners, but the 'new home' feeling wears off after time. But feelings are just that, feelings. We don't love our home based on a 'new home feeling'; we love it because God built it for us, and now we are in the next phase of home ownership, which is continued care for our home. We are invested in maintenance features; we make repairs when needed, and we continue to beautify our space with new furniture pieces and art.

I share this because your 'new home feeling' will also wane. It feels indescribable when you first accept Salvation through Jesus Christ and invite the Holy Spirit to live in your spiritual home! You feel God moving in your home and get excited about the new furniture pieces as you see God's design coming to life! After you put this book down, you will feel invigorated and ready to glorify God with your being; your *why* in life has come into focus, and you are ready to point others to God! However, I want to be honest and transparent with you; that excited feeling will fade over time. But here's the thing: you don't glorify God with your life because of a feeling. You do it because it is your purpose for being here; it is your response to God's purchase of you.

The Apostle Paul put it this way when speaking to the Ephesian church, "Therefore I, the prisoner in the Lord, *urge you* to walk worthy of the calling you received" (Ephesians 4:1, NIV). He told the Philippian church, "Just one thing: As citizens of heaven, live your life worthy of the gospel of Christ" (Philippians 1:27, CSB). On both of these occasions, Paul wanted Christ's followers to know they needed to live their lives in a way that was deserving of, suitable to, and in alignment with the gospel of Christ.

The gospel of Christ is the good news about Jesus Christ (The Way, The Truth, and The Life), what He has done for us (redeemed us to God), and what He is doing (being Lord in our lives). We don't rely on the 'new home feeling'. Instead, we pattern our lives after Jesus Christ so we can bear His image and glorify God with our being regardless of how we feel.

God Is Not Mocked

As we near the end of this book and you prepare to live your life full out for Jesus Christ, glorifying God with every part of your being, I must emphasize Galatians 6:7 (CSB), **"God is not mocked."** The Greek word for mock within this text is muktérizó, which means to sneer at, disregard, and disdain. Simply, God and His guiding principles should not be played with or ignored. In this specific text, the Truth that follows is about sowing and reaping, "Because the one who sows to his flesh will reap destruction from the flesh, but the one who sows to the Spirit, will reap eternal life from the Spirit" (Galatians 6:8, CSB). God is telling you right now: *Do not mock my words;* mark *my words. Do not disregard my instruction; heed it. You know your purpose now; your reason for being here is clear and in focus. DO NOT continue to sow, put stock in, work to feed, or have a vested interest in your flesh. If you do, you will reap destruction, the demolition of your faith, scarring in your spirit, ruin in your emotions, the shattering of your heart, the dismantling of your relationship with me (God), and the purpose of your life will be defeated. Instead, sow, give life to, throw yourself at, give all your energy to, and have a vested interest in the Spirit of God.*

Take a moment to breathe in those words from Father God. Do not close the book, do not take a reading break. Sit with the words your Father is speaking to you at this moment. Right now, you feel the pull of God's Spirit; do not let the gravitational pull of what is around you disrupt this holy moment. Decide at this moment where you will sow your time, your talents, your treasure. Determine right now and even say out loud that God will get all of you. Commit in your heart to give God and His Kingdom your undivided attention, and your actions will follow. Everything you read up to this moment will be for naught if you don't choose this day whom you will serve.

Joshua and the Israelites were at a similar decision point thousands of years ago. The Israelites, God's Chosen people, were recently freed from their oppressor, the Egyptians. Still, with their shackles loosed by God and their freedom in hand, the Israelites were on the fence about who they would serve. God released them from the bondage of slavery and the grip of their enslaver, and still, they were conflicted, undecided on who and what would get their affection. They were torn between the call to worship the Lord, and their desire to lord over themselves and worship created gods. At that moment, Joshua said, "Now therefore, fear the Lord, serve Him in sincerity and in truth, and put away the gods which your fathers served on the other side of the River in Egypt. Serve the LORD! And if it seems evil to serve the Lord, **choose for yourselves this day whom you will serve**, whether the gods which your fathers served that were on the other side of the River, or the gods of the Amorites, in whose land you dwell. But as for me and my house, we will serve the Lord" (Joshua 24:14-15, NKJV).

Do Not Weary in Doing Good

We want to believe we will stumble into sincerity in our Faith, sanctified living, and intimacy with God. But the truth is, we *choose* it. You make the choice today to serve God, to do good, to sow into a Spirit-filled life, and you repeat this choice every day as long as you are here on Earth. You will need to repeat this decision because temptation will try to beckon you away from the field of Faith and into the field of destruction. Sometimes, the temptation will be overt; you will be tempted to miss a church service, hang out with an immoral friend, watch the wrong television, engage in promiscuity, etc.

At other times, the temptation will be more covert. You will find yourself getting recognized and promoted at work; your children will thrive in their extracurriculars, and your relationship with your significant other will go to new heights and require more of you. While these subtle life changes are not bad, they are opportunities to divert your attention from God. They are subtle and seemingly harmless life details that, if you are not careful, will move you to sow into your flesh, your here and now, what you can see. The everyday temptation, the standing tactic of Satan, is to divert our affection from God because he (Satan) misplaced his affection for God and aimed to worship himself. Subsequently, Satan met destruction, and he wants the same destruction for you.

With that endgame in mind for you, the enemy persistently and recklessly works to deceive you into sowing into your flesh. He will use anything in this life, be it calamity or pleasure, to persuade you to move where you plant your seed—to cause you to put more effort and energy in the garden of your fleshly man rather than God's Spirit. Let me say it more clearly. "God is a Spirit: and they that worship *him* must worship Him in Spirit and in Truth" (John 4:24, KJV). You understand that, good. With that understanding, if you sow, invest in, and put all your efforts into your flesh, you cannot worship God because worship with Him happens in the Spirit. You are still following me, good.

When you cannot worship God, commune with Him, or experience Him, you are outside His presence. When you are outside of God's presence, you experience destruction. Our enemy, the devil, knows this full well because he fell from God's presence like lightning (Luke 10:18) and subsequently experienced destruction (Colossians 2:15). The enemy is serving an eternal life sentence of destruction and defeat. Now, he roams the Earth looking for people to devour (1 Peter 5:8). He is looking for people to serve the eternal life sentence of destruction with him.

You may be thinking: *Okay, I won't sow into my flesh because I don't want to face destruction here on Earth or in eternity.* Good, but let me be clear: the temptation to sow into your flesh will not be a one-and-done experience; you will be confronted with this temptation every day for the rest of your life.

The good news is Jesus, our Lord and Savior, the Word of God, wrapped himself in flesh so He could be tempted in all points and not sin (Hebrews 4:15). Jesus did not do this to prove that perfection is possible. We are not Jesus; we will sin, and He gives us grace for our sins. However, Jesus embraced a bodily form when he walked the earth as a man and He was subjected to the consistent temptation tactics the enemy uses to draw us away from the Father. Jesus gained victory over sin and temptation so we can live a victorious life!

The scriptures do not detail every specific temptation experienced across generations. With each passing year, the modality of temptation changes. With technology, our access to temptation and its access to us changes. However, the defined points and the categories of temptation remain the same. We will all be tempted when it comes to the lust of the flesh, the lust of the eyes, and the pride of life. First John 2:16 (NIV) states, **"For everything in the world- the lust of the flesh, the lust of the eyes, and the pride of life-comes not from the Father but from the world."** We need to know this fully and be on high alert against these temptation points in our spiritual home if we want to sow into the Spirit and glorify God with our life.

Jesus defeated this three-prong temptation tactic so we can experience freedom and a Spirit-filled life. Let's go to Luke 4 to dig deeper into Jesus' victory story. The account of Jesus' temptation is also covered in the gospels of Matthew and Mark, but we are going to dive into Luke's coverage of this story, which reads: "Then Jesus left the Jordan, full of the Holy Spirit, and was led by the Spirit in the wilderness" (Luke 4:1, CSB). Let's stop there for a moment. You may be wondering: *Why was Jesus at the Jordan?* I am glad you asked. Jesus was at the Jordan River because He was just baptized there. Luke 3:21-22 (CSB) says, "When all the people were baptized, Jesus was also baptized. As he was praying, heaven opened, and the Holy Spirit descended on him in a physical appearance like a dove. And a voice came from heaven: You are my beloved Son; with you I am well-pleased."

So, Jesus was baptized, He received the Holy Spirit, God affirmed him as His Son with whom He was well-pleased, and *then* the Holy Spirit led Jesus into the wilderness where the devil tempted him. This additional context on Jesus' recent baptism in the Holy Spirit is critical for you and me. Why? First, it points to the necessity of the Holy Spirit for *anyone* who is walking this Earth and pursuing a relationship with God through Jesus Christ. Jesus needed the Holy Spirit to dwell in His spiritual home because while He walked the Earth as man, He was wrapped in flesh. Yes, Jesus and God are one, but the fleshly man sought to gain access and authority over Jesus' home just like it aims to gain access in our spiritual homes today.

Secondly, Jesus' baptism in the Holy Spirit points to the truth that God is thoughtful and strategic. The first Adam, who we learned about in Chapter One of this book, succumbed to sin when tempted by Satan. When Adam ate the forbidden fruit, he didn't just make a poor meal choice. He gave into his fleshly desire to have what God said was off-limits (lust of the flesh). He ate the fruit despite God's instruction not to eat it because it looked pleasing to the eyes (lust of the eyes). Adam and his wife, Eve, were deceived into believing that when they ate the forbidden fruit, their eyes would be opened, and they would be like God, knowing good and evil (the pride of life). When Adam yielded to temptation–the lust of the flesh, the lust of the eyes, and the pride of life–he forfeited God's presence. He and Eve were banned from the Garden of Eden, and they experienced destruction, the demolition of their faith, scarring in their spirit, ruin in their emotions, the shattering of their heart, and the dismantling of their relationship with God. With their fall, every man and woman after them was born into that fallen, destructive state.

Now, God was going to allow the second Adam, His Son Jesus, to experience Satan's temptation. However, the strategy was different this time around. God was sending His Son, who He was one with, **and** His Holy Spirit, who is God's Spirit. You missed it; I missed it, too, as I was typing it. I will say it again. When Jesus was led into the wilderness to be tempted by Satan, God sent His Son, who He is one with, and the Holy Spirit, who is God's Spirit. In essence, God the Father, Jesus the Son, and the Holy Spirit went into the wilderness to be tempted by Satan. The Trinity was present as Jesus was being tempted! The three-part God took on the three-part temptation tactic-lust of the flesh, lust of the eyes, and the pride of life. If you are not shouting yet, keep reading. God sent His 'Big Three' to take on Satan's 'big three'. And you already know who was victorious!

Okay, stop shouting for a moment; let's go back to Luke 4:1-2 (CSB): "Then Jesus left the Jordan(river), full of the Holy Spirit, and was led by the Spirit into the wilderness for forty days to be tempted by the devil. He ate nothing during those forty days, and when they were over, he was hungry." Let's stop here for a moment. Jesus was in the wilderness for forty days, not eating. He was fasting. The Holy Spirit first led Jesus to the wilderness to fast, turn down His plate, and put His flesh under subjection to God's Spirit. This is an important callout because today, as followers of Jesus Christ, we have to live a life of fasting if we want to have the spiritual strength and stamina to overcome Satan's temptation in our lives. We have to allow God's Holy Spirit, who lives on the inside of us, to lead us into periods of fasting, where for some time we do not eat certain foods or food at all; a time where we turn down the noise of life, abstain from specific television programs, media channels, and instead dive deep into God's word and into prayer. Your time of fasting may not be forty days, or it may be. Your fasting time may be seven days or 21 days. Let God's Holy Spirit lead you on the time; you just follow the instructions when you hear them. Fasting is critical to every believer's spiritual health.

Jesus was one with God. He is a part of the Holy Trinity, but because he took on bodily form and was wrapped in flesh, He fasted to keep His flesh in order. He fasted to command His flesh, that is fed by this world's kingdom, to bow and bend to the Kingdom of God; His flesh could not have authority in His life.

After Jesus abstained from food for forty days, He was spiritually full but physically hungry. Let's keep reading. Luke 4:3-4 (CSB): "Then the devil said to him, 'If you are the Son of God, tell this stone to become bread.' But Jesus answered him, "It is written: Man must not live on bread alone." Satan's first temptation tactic was in the 'lust of the flesh' category. Satan understood Jesus' vulnerability in that moment; Jesus was physically hungry, and reasonably so. He did not eat food over a forty-day period. However, Jesus responded with God's Word and defeated the temptation to succumb to the hunger pangs from His flesh. You may wonder: *What harm would there be in Jesus exercising His power to produce food for himself? After all, hunger is a natural response to 40 days of fasting.* You are right, but Jesus took His instructions from His Father (God) and God's Spirit. He refused to entertain any instruction from His enemy. A secondary lesson we learn from Jesus is the wisdom to discern between what is good and what is God. Jesus knew that even if it sounded or felt like a good thing if it was not from God, it was not for Him. You have to have that same resolve.

You and I, like Jesus, have an enemy who studies us. He knows our weaknesses better than we do. He preys on our vulnerabilities, lies in wait, and seeks out opportune moments to tempt us, to compel us to sow into the flesh. He eagerly anticipates the moment when our guard is down, and we haven't been in God's presence. He presents us with temptation when the volume of life is at a fever pitch and when we are most distracted by life's calamities or pleasures.

Next, "The devil led him [Jesus] up to a high place and showed him in an instant all the kingdoms of the world. And he said to him, 'I will give you all the authority and splendor; it has been given to me and I can give it to anyone I want to. If you worship me, it will all be yours.' Jesus answered, 'It is written: Worship the Lord your God and serve him only' (Luke 4: 5-8, CSB). In this instance, Satan deployed the 'lust of the eyes' tactic. He *showed* Jesus, in an instant, the kingdoms of the world, expecting Jesus to be enticed by what he saw and hoping that Jesus would bow down and worship him.

This temptation tactic seems laughable when presented to Jesus, the Son of God, the one whose name is higher than any name above the Earth, on Earth, and below the Earth (Philippians 2:9). It was also quite foolish of Satan to think that Jesus would be enticed by the offer of authority in the kingdoms of this world when Jesus had all authority. "For in him all things were created: things in heaven and on earth, visible and invisible, whether thrones or powers or rulers or authorities; all things have been created through him and for" (Colossians 1:15-16, NIV). AND ultimately, the kingdoms of this world will become the kingdom of our Lord and his Messiah. He will reign forever and ever (Revelation 11:15). All that to say, Jesus had nothing to gain from Satan, yet Satan still tempted Him with the lust of the eyes; he compelled Jesus to misplace His worship for God to obtain Earthly possessions.

It is quite literally one of the oldest tricks in the book, but Satan still uses this same temptation tactic on you and me today. He still flashes the kingdom of this world in our faces; in an instant, we are tempted to worship what we see. Today's society is a breeding ground for this type of temptation. Every day, we are bombarded with images of a better life or body, ways to get richer, and steps to finding the man or woman of our dreams. These flashy images and false advertisements are designed to draw our eyes to what is shiny, seductive, and shallow, so we will invest our time, money, and heart into the kingdom of this world while devaluing and disregarding the Kingdom of our God. We talked about the Kingdom of God earlier. Our spiritual home resides in the Kingdom of our God; we cannot glorify God if we are fixated on, enamored with, and devoted to the things of this world. James 4:4 (NIV) says it directly, "You adulterous people, don't you know that friendship with the world means enmity (hatred) against God? Therefore, anyone who chooses to be a friend of the world becomes an enemy of God."

Finally, Satan's third temptation appeal to Jesus came in the form of the pride of life. Let's go back to the scripture. Luke 4:9-13 (NIV) reads: "The devil led him [Jesus] to Jerusalem and had him stand on the highest point of the temple. 'If you are the Son of God,' he said, 'throw yourself down from here. For it is written: 'He will command his angels concerning you to guard you carefully; they will lift you up in their hands so that you will not strike your foot against a stone.' Jesus answered, 'It is said: Do not put the Lord your God to the test.' When the devil had finished all this tempting, he left him until an opportune time."

There is *so* much to unpack in this final temptation sequence. First, notice how Satan led Jesus to Jerusalem, to the highest point of the temple. Satan led Jesus to a holy place. Jesus was no longer in the wilderness. The location of this temptation is important for you and me to note and be cognizant of because it matters. Too often, we expect Satan's temptations to show up in wilderness seasons in our lives, in those moments when our spiritual life is dry, or we are physically or emotionally in despair. But sometimes Satan presents us with the temptation to deny God or distance ourselves from His presence when we are in a good place, life is going well, things are working in our favor, and in moments where our relationship with God is at its strongest. Jesus was at a sacred, sanctified location when Satan deployed his final temptation. Let that serve as notice to you and me that we can never let our guard down.

Let's keep unpacking this. So, Jesus is at the holy place when Satan tells him to throw himself down from the highest point in the temple. It is important to note that Jesus changed location. He was in a high, holy location, but Satan also changed his approach. When Satan tempted Jesus the previous two times, Jesus responded with the Word of God. So this time, Satan proactively offered scripture to Jesus before Jesus could respond with the Word of God. Satan knows scripture; he knows more scripture than most believers. He put his knowledge on display when he told Jesus, "For it is written: He will command his angels concerning you to guard you carefully; they will lift you up in their hands so that you will not strike your foot against a stone" (Luke 4:10, NIV). Satan is cunning, crafty, and convoluted. He will twist and distort the truth–to include God's word–to make it align with his schemes. You should know that, like Jesus, when you are walking out holiness and are glorifying God with your life, Satan will adjust his approach to meet you at your new level.

Satan encouraged Jesus to throw himself down from the highest point in the temple, but he led with, "*If* you are the Son of God." He was trying to bait Jesus into falling into temptation by pulling on the lever of pride, which exists in every fleshly being. Satan wanted Jesus to feel compelled to show off his strength and flex his spiritual muscles. Satan wanted Jesus to feel inclined to prove Himself because the root of all pride is insecurity. Oh, you thought pride was merely arrogance or a flagrant obsession for oneself. Not so much. Pride manifests outwardly as bravado, but its origin is deep self-consciousness, self-doubt, anxiety around how others perceive you, or an unhealthy interest in controlling how others perceive you. Pride is a symptom of living flesh. Humility is evidence of flesh that has been put to death by Jesus Christ.

Pride can also be arrogance and bravado and it is worth noting that the temptation to be prideful in this manner shows up most often when we are in a holy place, and, believe it or not, we are most likely to let our guards down when we feel most secure in our faith. It is not uncommon for pride to present itself when life is working out, and things are going well. It is then that we feel most tempted to step away from our prayer closets, shorten our time in God's word, and loosen our dependence on God because "we got this." Pride also comes to a head when we agree with the foolish idea that "we have arrived" in our Faith and are tempted to look down on others who "just can't get it together."

Not only was Satan pulling on the pride-lever that existed within Jesus' flesh, but he was also trying to get Jesus to test His Father and misuse His heavenly resources, " Throw yourself down from here...for it is written, He (God) will command his angels concerning you to guard you carefully..." Satan wanted Jesus to put God in a precarious position as a result of Jesus' reckless decision-making. Pride will make you do that. Pride, regard for oneself, and ego will push you to act outside of God's will and dare God to rescue you from your self-inflicted downfall. However, Jesus did not fall for that form of temptation. Jesus was bent on remaining at the top, at His holy place (literally and spiritually). He also refused to yield to pride and demonstrate reckless abandon in His Faith or life. We must have this same resolve.

We spent time gaining an understanding of Satan's big three, the lust of the flesh, the lust of the eyes, and the pride of life because these types of temptations *will* show up in your life. It is not *if* they show up; it is *when* they show up. When they show up and seek to dominate your spiritual home, you need to remember that Satan's 'big three' were defeated by God's 'Big Three.' The material Satan uses to tempt us will vary; he customizes temptation for each person, but the desired outcome is the same for all of us. He wants us to sow into the field of our flesh. The enemy plants seeds of temptation in the forms of the lust of the flesh, the lust of the eyes, and the pride of life so we can water them and ultimately produce their destructive fruit. But you will not sow into your flesh; you will sow into the Spirit and glorify God with all your being.

Be Holy

When you choose to sow into the Spirit, pursue the Kingdom of God, pattern yourself after Jesus, and pursue a life of righteousness, you choose holiness. For some, when you see the word holiness, you immediately envision the 'old school' church with wooden pews, tambourines, a booming organ, church mothers in white, and ushers standing guard at the door. For some, when you think about holiness, you immediately think about stifled pleasures, dashed dreams, a stuffy life, and a list of 'dos and don'ts. Holiness in its purest state is godliness. God is holy, divine, sanctified, virtuous, pure, without sin—God is perfect. Because God is holy, we aim to live a life of holiness. We sow seed into the Spirit, pursue a relationship with God through Jesus, and subscribe to Kingdom-living in our spiritual homes because we want to be holy.

First Peter 1:13-17 (NIV) tells us about holiness, "Therefore with your minds ready for action, be sober-minded and set your hope completely on the grace to be brought to you at the revelation of Jesus Christ. As obedient children do not be conformed to the desires of your former ignorance. But as the one who called you is holy, you are also to be holy in all your conduct, for it is written: **Be holy, because I (God) am holy** (1 Peter 1:16, CSB). There is so much to unpack from just these few scriptures.

First, Peter sets the stage for holiness with a call to be sober-minded. When you think about sobriety, you likely make the connection to alcoholic drinks, and that is a fine parallel and helpful reference point. To be sober is to be clear-headed, not drunk, abstinent. Peter is telling us if you want to be holy, you have to be clear-headed, focused on Jesus, and on living a life of grace. You cannot be drunk off the culture of this world, still enamored with it and chasing the desires of your former life. You cannot be in pursuit of the things of the kingdom of this world and the Kingdom of God. You must be abstinent; you must abstain from worldviews and philosophies that seek to cloud your judgment and weaken your sensitivity to God's Spirit. You must be holy, sanctified, and pure because your God is Holy.

Holiness **is not** about being perfect like God; it is the pursuit of being more like God every day. God understands that we contend with our flesh and the enemy daily. He understands the war for our soul that is underway every moment of every day. With that, He extends grace when we miss the mark of Holiness; we are in a faulty earth suit, and God gets that. Still, as a follower of Jesus Christ and as one who is committed to glorifying God with our entire being, holiness is our daily objective. Every morning, we pursue holiness; we wake up, thank God for the new day, for breathing His breath into our nostrils once again, and for gifting us with another opportunity to give Him glory. We approach each day we are given on this Earth with a hunger and thirst for holiness. We pray to God and dive deep into His written Word because we want to trace His steps so we can follow Him and live a life of holiness. We want to pick up God's scent so we can be His aroma on Earth and reflect holiness. We turn over every stone in scripture to find His character so we can emulate Him. We humble ourselves before God so we can worship His Holiness. We strip ourselves of ourselves so we can be holy.

Holiness is bigger, deeper, and broader than a style of church service. It is more robust, enlightening, and powerful than doctrine or a list of dos and don'ts. Holiness is godliness; when we seek to be holy, we seek to align our life with the God who gave us life.

Shining Like Stars

Over the last three years, we have had several third parties come into our new home, whether it was the person who came to deliver a piece of furniture, an electrician who needed to address an electrical issue that was missed in the final walk-through of the home, or a maintenance technician who needed to fix an issue with the air conditioning system, etc. What is true for all of these visitors is they usually comment on how nice the inside of our home looks. They note the fixtures and furniture pieces, and some have gone as far as to ask if we purchased the builder's model home. They ask this because the aesthetics, the features of the homes, and the design of our homes are beautiful and well-kept.

Why do I share this? The spiritual home God is building on the inside of you should reflect the gospel of Jesus Christ so that it draws attention from others. It is not about being flashy or excessive; it is about living like God, modeling our lives after God to the point where we look like Him, and it is so attractive that others take notice.

Philippians 2:13-15 (NIV) says, "For it is God who is working *in you* to will and to work according to his good purpose. Do everything without grumbling and arguing so that you may be blameless and pure children of God without fault in a warped and crooked generation. Then you will shine among them like stars in the sky." God is working on the inside of your spiritual home. He is ensuring that your life lines up with His will and good purpose for your life. He is setting your home apart, so in this world that is dying, full of chaos, dominated by culture, and depraved, you shine like a star. You shine like a star so people can be drawn to the light of Jesus Christ.

Shining like a star is your calling and cannot be based on feelings. Jesus reinforces our calling in the book of Matthew when he told his disciples, "You are the light of the world. A town built on a hill cannot be hidden. Neither do people light a lamp and put it under a bowl. Instead, they put it on a stand, and it gives light to everyone in the house. In the same way, let your light shine before others, that they may see your good deeds and *glorify your Father in heaven"* (Matthew 5:14-16).

Glorifying God is the point; it is our high calling and our responsibility as citizens of heaven who reside here on Earth. We were purchased with a very specific purpose: to make sure we glorify God with our beings. We don't wait for a feeling or a 'want to.' We will ourselves to glorify God with our lives because that is our why; that is the sole purpose that we are here. Everything else in our lives becomes a secondary function and responsibility to the primary goal of glorifying God with our lives every day.

Now that you know why you are here, you must be intentional with every moment you have and every breath you are given. Your spiritual home has to be your priority; this ensures that Jesus is the Lord of your life and that He controls you, which has to be your daily objective. Making sure that God's Spirit has space and free course on the inside so you can reflect God on the outside has to be your life's mission.

The Apostle Paul said it like this, "Not that I have already obtained all of this, or have already arrived at my goal, but I press on to take hold of that for which Christ Jesus took hold of me. Brothers and sisters, I do not consider myself yet to have taken hold of it. But one thing I do: Forgetting what is behind and straining toward what is ahead, I press on toward the goal to win the prize for which God has called me heavenward in Christ Jesus" (Philippians 3:12-14, NIV).

We all must be committed to the press that Paul describes when speaking to the Philippian church. It is a daily push towards the mark— the goal of looking like Jesus and glorifying God with our being. It is a marathon, not a sprint, and we have to make sure we are disciplined and that spiritual training is taking place in our spiritual homes. We condition ourselves by engaging with God and His truth, applying God's truth in our life, and building our faith muscles so we win the prize in this life, we glorify God with our being, and most importantly, we win the eternal prize of life with God when this earthly life is over.

The Apostle Paul says, "Do you not know that in a race, all runners run, but only one gets the prize? Run in such a way as to get the prize. Everyone who competes in the games goes into *strict training*. They do it to get a crown that will not last, but we do it to get a crown that will last forever. Therefore, I do not run like someone running aimlessly; I do not fight like a boxer beating the air. No, I strike a blow to my body and make it my slave so that after I have preached to others, I myself will not be disqualified for the prize" (1 Corinthians 9:24-27, NIV).

It is time to stop wandering through your life aimlessly, running after what is in front of you but getting nowhere fast. It is time to start walking in your divine purpose. You are here because God SO loved you and saw so much value in you that He purchased you with His Son's blood. You are here because God wants to live on the inside of you, effect change in your life, and empower you. It is time to declare and stand on the declaration daily, "As for me and my house we will serve the Lord" (Joshua 24:15, NKJV). You are here to glorify God with your body and entire being, so from this moment forward, do just that!

AFTERWORD

This book was not intended to be a one-time read. The truth of God's Word woven throughout each letter of this book is powerful, and He does not want you to just read and proceed with your life as usual. Go back and re-read the chapters of this book, track down the scripture references, and study those verses. Let this book be a complimentary tool during your prayer and study time.

ABOUT THE AUTHOR

Porcia Wade is a Truth seeker and teacher. She is a student of God's Word whose mission is to present God to people in a real, relatable, and reliable way as she writes books, teaches, and leads small group discussions. Porcia believes that a relationship with God through Jesus is the only way to gain eternal life and capture a higher quality of life (peace, provision, and joy) in the here and now.

God has blessed her with a ministry that also includes being a wife, mother, and working professional. Porcia is an everyday woman who wants to point people to an extraordinary God!

www.ingramcontent.com/pod-product-compliance
Lightning Source LLC
Chambersburg PA
CBHW051633120626
46551CB00014B/2067